Global Financial Integration:
The End of Geography

CHATHAM HOUSE PAPERS

An International Economics Programme Publication
Programme Director: J. M. C. Rollo

The Royal Institute of International Affairs, at Chatham House in London, has provided an impartial forum for discussion and debate on current international issues for some 70 years. Its resident research fellows, specialized information resources, and range of publications, conferences, and meetings span the fields of international politics, economics, and security. The Institute is independent of government.

Chatham House Papers are short monographs on current policy problems which have been commissioned by the RIIA. In preparing the papers, authors are advised by a study group of experts convened by the RIIA, and publication of a paper indicates that the Institute regards it as an authoritative contribution to the public debate. The Institute does not, however, hold opinions of its own; the views expressed in this publication are the responsibility of the author.

CHATHAM HOUSE PAPERS

Global Financial Integration: The End of Geography

Richard O'Brien

The Royal Institute of International Affairs

Pinter Publishers
London

© Royal Institute of International Affairs, 1992

First published in Great Britain in 1992 by
Pinter Publishers Limited
25 Floral Street, London WC2E 9DS

British Library Cataloguing in Publication Data

A CIP catalogue record for this book is available from the British Library

ISBN 1-85567-005-4 (Paperback)
      1-85567-004-6 (Hardback)

Reproduced from copy supplied by
Koinonia Limited
Printed and bound in Great Britain by
Biddles Ltd

CONTENTS

ACKNOWLEDGMENTS

I am indebted to all those who have taken the time to read drafts of this study and discuss the issues at length. I cannot thank them all individually: their number is too great to list here and I would not wish to implicate anyone by suggesting their endorsement of my views. However, I do wish to thank Jim Rollo of the Royal Institute of International Affairs, at Chatham House, for encouraging me to persevere with such an ambitious task, which develops at length my short essay 'The End of Geography', first published in *The AMEX Bank Review*. I am also greatly indebted to the members of the Chatham House study group that discussed earlier drafts, and to my colleagues at American Express Bank for their comments and criticisms. The short bibliography acknowledges how much good work has already been carried out on the subject, even if I have not done justice to all the thoughts and analyses available in these works.

It is my hope that this study will at least stimulate further thinking on the changing dimensions of international and global finance. Integration requires a change in identity, whether for nations, peoples, markets or firms. It will always be tempting, when conditions get tough as a result of intense competition, to seek refuge in old identities. I hope this paper encourages market participants and policymakers to keep pressing for more imaginative ways of developing new identities based on more integrated markets and not to revert to type.

November 1991   Richard O'Brien

1

TOWARDS THE END OF GEOGRAPHY

The end of geography, as a concept applied to international financial relationships, refers to a state of economic development where geographical location no longer matters in finance, or matters much less than hitherto. In this state, *financial market regulators* no longer hold full sway over their regulatory territory: that is, rules no longer apply solely to specific geographical frameworks, such as the nation-state or other typical regulatory jurisdictional territories. For *financial firms*, this means that the choice of geographical location can be greatly widened, provided that an appropriate investment in information and computer systems is made: for example, 'back office' functions may be in one location, sales forces may be spread widely across the marketplace, and the legal domicile of the firm may be elsewhere. The firm can operate wherever the markets and factors of production happen to be. *Stock exchanges* can no longer expect to monopolize trading in the shares of companies in their country or region, nor can trading be confined to specific cities or exchanges. Stock markets are now increasingly based on computer and telephone networks, not on trading floors. Indeed, markets almost have no fixed abode. For *the consumer of financial services*, the end of geography means that a wider range of services will be offered, outside the traditional services offered by local banks. 'Global choice' might be the ambitious watchword of the users of financial services in the late twentieth century. The end of geography threatens cartels and clubs as new products and services enter protected markets. The price of capital is becoming the same everywhere, at least in wholesale markets. The end of geography is a challenge to all participants in the world economy, to developing as well as developed economies, to public and private policymakers, to producers and consumers of financial services. It involves the debate over the role of the nation-state, the integration of nations and the disintegration of existing federations.

There will be forces seeking to maintain geographical control: regulators and financial firms will continue to protect and define their geographical territory, their 'turf' and their market share. The debate over European union reveals many examples of efforts to defend geography – or what in this context is often termed 'sovereignty' – despite the diminished sovereignty of nations in an integrated world economy. Differences between markets and products are not about to disappear: indeed, product differentiation will intensify, as standard trade theory and practice has demonstrated. The structure of banking is not about to homogenize rapidly towards some standard norm while cultural and other differences remain. Intense battles are now being waged among stock exchanges, delaying the march towards 'seamless' markets and other such grand concepts. Retail banking networks will still rely on close proximity to the customer, although the extent to which the end of geography is happening in retail finance as well should not be underestimated: it is by no means a trend confined to wholesale business. All operations and people will have to have a location, a set of geographical coordinates. Many location decisions also have a deliberate geographical rationale, such as the booking of business in offshore financial centres for tax reasons, tax jurisdiction being a particularly 'geographical' concept. Geography will remain one of the most powerful, evocative and obvious reference points. Identities are rarely given up if there are no clear identities emerging in their place. Location will continue to matter while physical barriers exist, while travel still takes time, and while cultural and other social differences persist.

Yet, as markets and rules become integrated, the relevance of geography and the need to base decisions on geography will alter and often diminish. Money, being fungible, will continue to try to avoid, and will largely succeed in escaping, the confines of the existing geography.

The scope of the study

As befits an ambitious concept such as the end of geography, this survey sweeps through many aspects of international finance, economics and politics. It is not an analytical paper, in the sense of measuring in statistical terms the correlations and other numerical measures of integration and globalization; the aim is to try to derive some sense of policy priorities and choice from the broad, interlinked sets of issues.

This study involves many trends of the late twentieth century: computerization, deregulation, securitization, institutionalization, innovation and integration. In the chapters that follow, I shall distinguish between such geographical notions as domestic, international, multinational, cross-border, offshore and global. Chapters 2 and 3 discuss two key forces driving the financial world towards the end of geography: the changes in information technology (IT) and regulatory change. Both forces are particularly powerful in the financial context, given that money and its functions derive from the existence of money as an item of information, its role being designed by custom and regulation. Chapters 4 and 5 describe the experiences gained so far in building global markets in two particular areas: the eurocurrency markets and the development of a more global securities industry. I then go on (Chapter 6) to show why globalization in retail financial markets must not be ignored, even if much of the excitement to date has been in the wholesale sector. Chapter 7 gives attention to location questions vis-à-vis the end-of-geography state, especially in terms of the location of financial centres and financial firms, and their structures as global, regional or local firms. Chapter 8 investigates the European integration experience, where most of the ideas in the paper can be put to the test, and where the combination of macro and micro change is seen most vividly. Chapter 9 examines the links between the end of geography in finance and the wider process of economic and political integration. And, finally, the study closes with policy conclusions and priorities from this diverse set of interrelated discussions (Chapter 10).

All these issues are becoming of even greater interest in the more sober 1990s as a more questioning approach to globalization is being expressed. After the boom-finance days of the 1980s, when going global was all the rage, some observers forecast a return to domestic bases and less enthusiasm for global firms and services. Meanwhile in the economics field the ambitious integration process in Europe is reaching its most testing period, and the natural enthusiasms unleashed in Eastern Europe in 1989 are being partly dampened by the enormity of the reform task. The 1980s saw a major sea-change towards liberalization and deregulation, 'allowing the market to decide'. The fallout from that period is encouraging a reassessment of that approach.

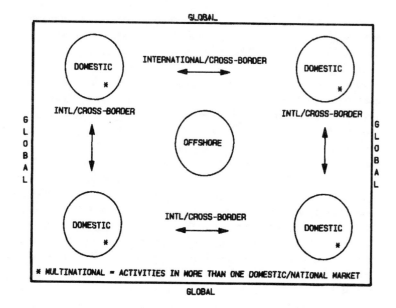

Figure 1 Diagrammatic representation of geographical concepts

Defining geographical terms

Before embarking on the rest of the analysis, it is worth clarifying a few geographical terms. These terms are used to describe markets, economies, products, services, firms, regulators and supervisors, and consumers. The various concepts are described diagrammatically in Figure 1.

Domestic refers to the environment within a single economy (in the diagram, in one or more of the four sample nations). Domestic business refers to the business conducted in the same market as the domicile of the firm or customer, for the most part being the place where taxes are paid and where the majority of ownership lies. It will also usually mean where business is conducted in the same currency as the base currency of the firm. The domestic market is also that which is presided over by the national regulators and government. Terms such as resident and non-resident are used to define differences between domestic and foreign. The end of geography itself blurs the precise boundaries between domestic and other (foreign) business: indeed, all geographical terms become harder to define and at the extreme become meaningless.

International means activities taking place between nations. International finance refers to financial flows or services between nations, although it is regularly used to describe any business that is not wholly domestic. If nations did not exist there would be no '*inter*-national' concept.

Multinational describes activities taking place in more than one nation. A bank or company, for example, may be multinational by operating in more than one nation. Being multinational does not necessarily involve a great deal of international business: a multinational's operations can be confined to domestic business in those places in which it has a presence. Of course, most multinational businesses and banks will carry out international transactions as well as operate in local markets. Furthermore, a multinational may have a strong international business structure and network, including multinational sourcing of materials, networking technology, expertise and clients. Often the whole purpose of the multinational presence will be to operate in other countries, behind national boundaries and barriers, as well as to offer international and cross-border services.

Cross-border is almost synonymous with international and often will be a preferable term, in that it is less likely to be confused with global or multinational. It is another way of expressing the sense '*inter*-national'.

Offshore refers to activities that are outside some specific jurisdictions (albeit onshore somewhere else).

Global should refer to operations within an integral whole, if it is to have a separate meaning from the foregoing terms. Global combines the elements of international and multinational with a strong degree of integration between the different national parts. The term is much misused: it may refer to a multinational presence, but if that merely involves a multiple domestic presence in many countries, then the term multinational may be more precise and accurate. International operations are often called global, but if the national distinction is still important, without the added integration between the national or otherwise separated markets or sectors, then again the term international is appropriate.

There are a limited number of services, markets, systems, products and firms that can be termed truly global. Usually international or multinational will be more correct, even though less attractive as advertising copy. A truly global service knows no internal boundaries, can be offered throughout the globe, and pays scant attention to national aspects. The nation becomes irrelevant, even though it will still exist. The closer we get to a global, integral whole, the closer we get to the end of geography.

The factors determining whether or not a global service can be offered depend on the existence, or otherwise, of exchange controls and separate currencies, the ability of the firm to trade in the various markets, and the number of locations in which the client has interests. Where there are barriers, products often have to be designed to overcome them, so that the global service can be offered despite the market segmentation or inefficiencies (the travellers cheque product is a good example).

What we have seen in the past few years is that financial firms may begin to think of themselves as global long before markets are global. Firms sell products as global products, even if these products are being sold into segmented national and regional markets. In recent years, for example, the idea of marketing global products became the fashion, following the thinking of management and marketing guru Theodore Levitt. The fashion is fading a little, not so much because the idea of a global product is inappropriate as such, but because often a product can be treated as global only if it sells into a global market, through global organizations. The product is invariably part of its environment. New regulations that allow global marketing do not, for example, create global products overnight, or global product acceptance. A British bank may be able to sell mortgages to Italian consumers, but that does not mean that it will be easy to out-compete those products that will appeal to local consumer preferences.

With these geographical concepts and distinctions in mind, it is now time to move on to examine the forces driving towards the end of geography in finance.

2

INFORMATION TECHNOLOGY AND GLOBAL FINANCE

Money is an 'information' product. The very essence of money is not so much in its physical appearance as in the information it conveys, whether as a debt, a store of value or a medium of exchange. Its universality depends upon the fact that everyone knows what money means, or can mean, even if it takes skills to manage it, to manipulate it, to use it. Money can exist in a physical state, or it can exist as an item of information, a record in a ledger, or even in an unwritten understanding between people or organizations. As soon as money goes beyond its physical state, its information characteristics come into play. Access to money depends on access to that information. Its existence as an information item also gives money its flexibility and its 'fungibility', the ability to be transferred from place to place, to move from purpose to purpose.

Any change in the way in which information is processed and delivered will influence the role of money: hence the radical change being experienced by information technology (IT) today is having a powerful impact on the role of money in the world economy. The importance of IT also derives from its exogenous nature, from its pervasive effect throughout the financial world and from its irreversibility. New technologies are here to stay, even though they are by no means uniformly applied and can become rapidly outdated as a result of even newer inventions and applications, involving the development of both hardware and software. The economics of financial services are being radically revised as a result of the reductions in costs associated with the new technology. New IT, being rapidly introduced into the financial services industry, affects communications systems, the speed of calculation and computation, and relationships between client and producer, among traders and between

7

markets themselves. As new technology allows information to move faster around the globe in new forms, so money can also move faster and in more mysterious ways. To a great extent the end-of-geography story is a technology story, the story of the computerization of finance.

From pigeon post to the green screen

Changes in communications have always had a profound effect, whether in finance or in any other walk of life. For example, some regard the laying of the transatlantic cable in 1866 as one of the most important events in the history of international economic integration and inter-dependence. Nathan Mayer Rothschild's use of carrier pigeons to bring him advance news of the result of the Battle of Waterloo is a legendary anecdote in the history of communications and finance. The present-day changes in the dimensions of communication – the speed, quality and 'depth' of communication that is now possible worldwide – are just as revolutionary.

The power of these dimensional changes is seen in the applications of the new technology: in wholesale finance, the switching of markets from trading floors to computer screens is changing the physical dimension of the marketplace and the relationships between traders and among the regulators of the markets; in retail finance, the introduction of automatic transfer machines (ATMs) and electronic points of sale (EFTPOS) opens up whole new dimensions for the delivery of financial services and may in part even lead to a radical reappraisal of the physical 'bricks and mortar' requirements of banks (long renowned for extensive branch outlets and the grandeur of their banking halls). The revolution has a long way to go, as is shown in the slow but gradual introduction of telephone banking and interactive screen communications between bank, retail seller and customer, which have long pointed to a future of screen-based shopping. The future will be significantly altered by the use of debit cards and even 'smart' cards (which store information in a micro-chip in the card), adding an extra dimension to the already proliferating use of 'plastic money' – an 'old' innovation, taken for granted but still in a rapid expansion and development phase.

One of the most important changes in the dimensions of communica-tions is that of speed; in many cases instant communication is now possible. In the context of the end of geography, the impact that this has on the relevance of location is particularly important. Market participants need not be in the same country or even on the same continent to be trading together. Even though the world will never be able to eliminate the fact that there are primarily three major time zones, technology now enables us to develop 24-hour trading in more and more areas (foreign exchange dealers have long been passing their own book around the globe on a continuous 24-hour basis).

The speed of communications has an equally important impact on the treatment of risk and exposures. As with all change, the impact can be felt in opposite directions at the same time: transactions that were once regarded as spot transactions, thus not involving settlements risks, now have to be re-examined even if the delay is only a few seconds, since almost any settlements delay, especially in those transactions involving millions of dollars of potential exposure, has to be watched and defined carefully (and measurement of exposure itself is becoming more complex); meanwhile, faster settlements systems can turn what were once long periods of exposure into short, almost spot, transactions. The efforts being made to improve settlements procedures all revolve around the timing of settlement as the critical factor that influences the size and scope of risk.

More extensive communication also brings markets and positions closer together. Assets and liabilities, involving a wider range of companies, transactions, currencies and markets, can be matched more rapidly across the globe, as the growth of the swap market testifies. With this greater speed of communication, access to instant information becomes even more critical for market competitiveness. The value of information deteriorates rapidly with time. Never has the old adage been more apt: time is money. A recent study reveals that a major investment in technology and systems gave one major US bank a ten-second advantage over other traders, a short but powerful time-gain worth billions of dollars if used properly to react to news ahead of the market (as reported in Hoekman and Sauvé, 1991). Again the impact can be felt in opposite ways: for example, the possibility of credit-card fraud has undoubtedly increased, but so also has the speed at which creditworthiness and identities can be checked. Meanwhile, no business has been left unchanged by the introduction of the fax machine, improving the quality and dimensions for rapid communication. Further advances continue, with the development, for example, of image processing (machines able to read documents and process them into digital form) and teleconferencing.

Mega-bytes on your lap

Alongside improved communications comes the quantum leap in the computing power now at the disposal of a wider and wider group of people. Allied to the new power of communicating information, these advances are a root cause behind the growing securitization of financial services. The ability of more players to process the information, which formerly could be kept and processed by only a limited group of players (i.e. banks), has reduced the barriers to entry into banking. At the same time, since information can be manipulated and communicated faster, more players can be involved: and more players means a deeper and more effective and competitive market (generally speaking). Even clients have the technology to follow the markets, keeping their financial advisers on their toes. Most dramatically perhaps, futures and options markets depend on 'rocket scientists' being able to handle large amounts of rapidly changing market data to calculate future prices and to balance opportunities and risks. All stock indices have long been dependent on a collection of prices being rapidly compiled: derivative markets require this data to be almost instantly transmitted elsewhere and products to be developed from it. These changes move the locus of business away from exchanges and basic cash markets. Indices of stock exchanges could not be traded on other markets without the new technologies being in place.

For some observers this introduction of hi-tech trading into the markets brings dangerous levels of instability, not least because of the increasing gap in understanding that often exists between the rocket scientists and those managing the markets or managing the firms that participate in the markets. Following the crash of 1987 there was a reappraisal, for example, of the wisdom of programme trading. In addition, as greater volumes of business develop away from the spot markets, the more potential there is for the tail to wag the dog. A breakdown in the flow of information as seen at the time of the crash, when trading had to stop because the stock ticker simply could not keep up with the volume of trade and of price changes, demonstrated the dependence of the markets on information and its timeliness. Of course technology can also be harnessed to cope with such problems, as in the introduction of circuit breakers to stop markets if volatility goes beyond a level deemed to be dangerous.

Technology must be applied

The impact of technology on the method and speed of communications and calculation gives the financial markets wholly new dimensions. But, despite the brave new world of instant end-of-geography communications across the globe, progress can be slowed by traditions, inertia and the more mundane problem of making the technology work as it is supposed to work. And, most important, new technologies do not introduce themselves: someone has to invest time, money and often reputations in technology. New technologies have undoubtedly reduced costs, but often the investment outlay is considerable. Even renting a Reuters screen can be expensive for the small financial adviser.

How fast will these innovations be introduced? The 'smart' card is an interesting example: it has been available for a long period but is only now being slowly introduced. Will innovations be acceptable to the user? How far must we consider a whole range of associated economic, social and political issues (e.g. privacy of information)? Clearly the use of new technology requires the acceptance of the new technology by customers and service providers, and requires a change in habits of operation, regulations and market structures. In the world of finance, where trust is a central element in all relationships, technology must be seen to work and not to place barriers between parties.

A classic example of the potential delays must be the fax machine, invented in the late nineteenth century but commercialized only in the past decade. The fax machine was an invention just waiting to be applied, waiting for the right combination of communication technology and economics to be developed at the right quality levels. Undoubtedly we will see increasing usage of the fax and increasing advances in the quality of the product. Perhaps its greatest importance will be in bringing *people* closer together: i.e., in bringing together those parts of the market in which issues are still discussed at length (as opposed to trading 'commodities'), and in which a rapid interactive exchange of information and views, either over the table or now over the fax machine, is still necessary. The disadvantage in not being in the room at the time is diminishing, although the ultimate advantage of physical contact will never disappear in a market which traditionally places a great premium, in certain areas, on the quality of people and personality. More interesting, however, than the fax machine's current impact may be its imminent fate: no sooner had the fax taken off than companies began investing in a new generation of products, using electronic mail (E-mail for short), which threatens to make the fax an outdated, expensive and slow piece of communications equipment.

The problem with periods of great technological advance is that they become caught up in their own momentum. While the market benefits from any major new advance, next year, often next week, there will be a more advanced product or system for sale. Thus, investing in technology can give rise to the most horrendous mistakes in terms of a firm's expense base. This is no new dilemma (witness the history of music-recording technology in recent years), but the speed at which one product can become outdated is accelerating, requiring even faster write-downs of any investment in equipment. Furthermore, there is a limited advantage in being ahead of one's time: since the marketplace has to accept the new technology, there is no point in having the most advanced communications technology if no one else is ready to receive the same input. These investment decisions are no less important in terms of software, which in effect defines the language that the market speaks, or the language used within an organization for internal communications.

The investor in new technology also has to be aware of the potential regulatory restrictions and other barriers to its introduction. Regulations police the storage and transfer of information. Regulators are acutely conscious of the potential privacy threats from technological advances, not to mention the sheer inconvenience of junk mail. It becomes an interactive process, with changes in regulation and in technology pursuing each other. Each advance in technology sets off a further round of inventions in technology and its application. New technology also depends on other capacities being available: mobile telephones are restricted in their growth by limitations in the number of airwaves, a problem that could be overcome in various ways, including the shifting of existing airwave users (such as TV) to cable, or even a new technological advance that somehow provides more airspace (just as fibre optic cable changed the whole range of capacities of cable communications). Investment in buildings for the financial sector must include a full awareness of communications technology needs and these change constantly. Today's trading firms have to be housed in major communications complexes.

Of course there is one force that will often help to accelerate the market's use of and investment in new technology: competition. In a fast-moving technology world no competitor can afford to be too far behind the competition or to invest in technology that is incompatible with that of the competition. Once a move into a new market is made, then the move can be very large and alter costs and profit margins quickly. For example, improvements in back-office technology have led to a rapid reduction in the profit margins in the global custody business (the holding of bonds and securities for clients for safekeeping), a business that is relatively straightforward yet also ripe for improvements in storage and other facilities. Where a saving can be made, investment will also come. A great deal of the consolidation of firms on Wall Street in the past twenty years has been driven by firms amalgamating and making large cost savings by using common back offices; the trend continues and is not confined to the securities trading business but also includes banks and other firms. At the time of change, however, delays in getting new technology to work, and in making it acceptable, can pose massive financial costs on those pursuing the change. For example, it is likely that the shift to a paperless stock record system such as the United Kingdom's TAURUS system points the way to the future, but delays in its introduction add to the costs, and there is always the fear that, by the time the system is in place, a whole redesign will be needed as a result of further advances in technology.—

Impact on market structures

The IT revolution has a major impact on the structure of financial markets and firms. One of the most intractable problems for financial markets is how banking systems that interact very differently with their respective corporate clients can work alongside each other in a globalized financial system, raising issues of 'system friction' (see Ostry, 1991). A key difference between the financial systems of the United States and those in, say, Germany and Japan is how information flows around the market, involving differences in approach to corporate governance, and different approaches to so-called insider trading.

Most obviously, the communications revolution alters the roles of different financial intermediaries by encouraging securitization. Banks are intermediaries, and their role is primarily one of making credit decisions based on the information available to them so that they can lend where the depositor has insufficient information to make that decision (the bank of course at the same time alters the short-term deposit into a longer-term loan). That information is stored primarily within the bank's own information system, even in the memory of its lending and credit officers, who develop a close knowledge of their customers. The quality of the bank's portfolio depends critically on the quality of that information and the use to which it is put by the bank. The loans are put on the bank's books: the bank takes the risk that its information is good, and having taken that risk, earns the reward for it. Often the information cannot be easily passed on outside the bank (or would not be made available to the bank by the customer if that information were to become public knowledge, available to competitors).

The information revolution has made the processing of both credit information easier and the communication of that information to a wider public both easier and cheaper. Selling the credit to the market is also easier and provides the borrower with a wider choice of lender. There may still remain an important category of privileged information which cannot be publicized, but financial intermediation through more open channels, through the marketplace, has become simpler and quite economical. The grip that the banks have over the credit assessment process has been reduced. Unfortunately for banks, the result has been that an increasing amount of good credit has been shifted to the traded securities markets, leaving the lower-quality credits for the banks, thereby reducing the average quality of banks' loan portfolios.

There still have to be ways for companies to share sensitive information with their banks. One of the benefits of the close corporate-bank relationships that have developed in German banking and elsewhere between companies and their investment banks has been to ensure that sensitive information can be exchanged without that knowledge being made instantly available to the market or to the firm's competitors. Private firms are private firms, but if they have market shareholders they have a public responsibility (to shareholders) to make reasonably full disclosure of information. Information is extremely valuable and is open to both misunderstanding and misuse. These are key issues in the question of the efficiency and effectiveness of the whole process of financial intermediation.

In short, the new information technologies have reduced the barriers to entry into core areas of banking by improving the market's ability to process information and by cutting the costs of information processing. The process opens up the issues of bank/client relations, of corporate governance and of the conduct of business vis-à-vis the sharing of information.

The potential new competitors for banks are not just the securities firms entering banking; rather, it is the providers of information technology themselves, Reuters and Telerate, that are becoming potential competitors, even though in practice the information companies also have to have access to the market information. In addition, one of the most important cross-industrial links may be between the information and telecommunications firms and the financial houses. It is possible that eventually specialization will restructure the markets yet again, with specialist information processors selling their services to the market makers, rather than trying to develop as trading firms themselves. At the retail end, new technology is gradually reducing the need for a physical presence in the high street and an ATM can be placed anywhere to sell any services (even before we enter the realms of telephone banking and screen shopping).

Where are we 'on the curve'?

Where are financial markets today on the curve in terms of the techno-logical advances being made and their application? We have had such a spate of invention and product development (the fax, ATMs, the mobile phone, screen-based trading systems and the personal computer, to name just five) that the next decade may well be primarily one of consolidation (which does not necessarily mean stability). The con-solidation phase might consist of the following aspects. First, on the technology side the main advances will be in terms of reducing the costs of the existing technologies and widening their acceptability and universality: a fax in every home alongside the telephone, etc. Second, the regulatory side will be catching up (e.g. the development of better settlements systems to cope with the new risks). Third, specialization may develop in the marketplace as financial firms decide which of the various types of service they can offer: overbanked countries such as the United States will consolidate their banking systems; the number of players trying to be global securities firms will settle down; and the exchanges will decide what structure they want to develop. At the retail end of banking, the massive overhang of property (i.e. high street locations) will have to be tackled as such locations change their roles (though the speed at which customers are switching to such facilities as ATMs can be exaggerated). Meanwhile, the world of dealmaking will still find a place for the physical contact provided by financial centres, such as the City of London. Yet even the physical description of the City is altering: no longer is the City synonymous with the Square Mile, since it now extends to Docklands and the West End. Even a revival in regional stockbroking can be discerned. Senior bankers will still want to meet, but their choice of meeting-place multiplies: they can travel to Frankfurt knowing that their office support and files are only a fax away.

Improved communications result in changes of location in two apparently opposite directions: it becomes less necessary for market participants to congregate in a single place (e.g. a single financial centre), but it also offers the opportunity to concentrate expertise in one place, given that products can be more easily disseminated from the centre. In other words, there is the possibility not only of concentration and centralization but also of dispersion and decentralization. This is not illogical: it means that location decisions are less restricted by communications issues, and other economies of scale can be exploited.

3

THE REGULATORY REVOLUTION

The role of money is defined by custom and ultimately in law. Regulatory regimes cover specific areas of jurisdiction, often coincident with specific geographical areas. Without regulations and an accepted regulatory structure, money can hardly perform any of its tasks. When the rule of law collapses, money in its customary form also collapses and may even become worthless: refugees from a collapsing regime traditionally see gold and precious items as a store of value and a future means of exchange, reverting to items that have a universal value beyond the scope of the collapsing regulatory structure, or the by then worthless 'promises to pay the bearer'.

Regulation issues are particularly important in the context of this paper because regulations are changing so rapidly today, from the broad move towards liberalization and deregulation in economic management – including the reduction in the role of the state in the economy – through to more specific changes in the regulation of finance. At the forefront of the liberalization process has been the effort to let the market decide on the allocation and pricing of economic resources. As far as the end-of-geography concept is concerned, the most vivid manifestation of this greater freedom has been the liberalization of capital flows across borders. In eliminating exchange and capital controls, governments are not only recognizing the power of capital integration (the end of geography in finance), but spurring the process on. Meanwhile, in each of the major financial markets – Japan, the United States and Europe – there are substantial programmes of regulatory reform under way. These changes lead to a significant redefinition of the role of money and of financial intermediaries.

It is also in the area of regulation that the major policy issues emerge from the end-of-geography challenge. Are regulators ready for the end of geography? Does the end of geography lead towards a global regulatory system and global rules?

The liberalization movement

Late-twentieth-century deregulation and liberalization began in the financial arena with the collapse of Bretton Woods in 1971, the removal of controls over the movement of money across borders and the removal of existing controls over the pricing of money (interest-rate deregulation). The seeds of this change were sown in the 1960s as the Bretton Woods system came under increasing strain. But it was not until the 1980s that the broader liberalization process in the wider arena of the political economy began to take off, under the political leadership of the United States and the United Kingdom. The North Atlantic, Anglo-Saxon alliance, reinforced by the Reagan/Thatcher mutual admiration society, led what was to become a worldwide deregulatory movement, involving a shake-up of labour practices (whether US air controllers or British miners), reduction of taxes, privatization, and the encouragement of the market to take the lead and decide the direction of resource flows, value, price and even acceptable practice. The process also implied a reduction in the role of government and the intention to reduce budget deficits, the latter being more successfully achieved in the United Kingdom than in the United States. In Europe also, the 1980s saw a crusade against burgeoning budget deficits, most dramatically forcing France's new socialist government to perform an acrobatic about-turn. Again, much of the groundwork creating the climate for change was laid in the 1970s, and the action then took place 'when the time was ripe'.

The respective roles of the United States and the United Kingdom in this process were complementary. The supply-side revolution and Reagan's brand of liberalism had to be of critical importance, given the size of the US economy (still the largest in the world despite the rise of Japan). In finance, the 1980s opened with US financial institutions still the largest players, especially in the international arena. Even today, despite being overtaken in size by Japanese firms, US firms and markets retain a certain dominance in terms of leading the market in innovation.

As to the United Kingdom contribution, Thatcherism undoubtedly played a vigorous supporting role, providing what economists like to call a 'demonstration effect'. In the financial arena, the importance of the

United Kingdom in this process was enhanced by the role of London as the world's pre-eminent international financial centre. London's 'Big Bang' in 1986 was an international phenomenon, in contrast to New York's much more parochial 'May Day' revolution in 1975 (when negotiable commissions were introduced on the New York Stock Exchange). London continues to retain considerable leadership characteristics, despite being under attack not least because of the impact of the end of geography. That this liberalization drive did not stop London itself developing one of the world's most cumbersome processes of regulatory reform serves as a reminder of the potential gaps that exist between theory and practice, between good intentions and final results.

Deregulation and liberalization clearly encourage globalization and integration. Liberal markets and systems tend to be open, providing greater ease of access, greater transparency of pricing and information. Transparency encourages the end of geography by revealing the cost of regulatory barriers – both discriminatory ones, imposed by national and other laws, and non-discriminatory ones, imposed by customs, cultures and market practices. Of course, revised regulations often end up providing new restrictions. But that is precisely the role of regulations: to define the limits of liberalization. The approach can differ: where the broad philosophy is one of liberalization (historically an Anglo-Saxon trait), the onus tends to be on the law to define where that liberal line *ends*; in a more restrictive climate, laws often define what *can* be done (reflected in the more dirigiste climate of France). The overall effect, none the less, is one of definition and limitation. There is always the risk that deregulation and liberalization can get out of hand, producing unforeseen adverse consequences and even chaos, especially where change is effected on a'piecemeal basis (often given the more acceptable label of sequencing). The outcome then is reregulation, just as repression is frequently the consequence of liberal political reform.

Regulatory change across the globe

Regulatory change in finance is happening in all major areas and sectors across the globe, even if not in a global framework (an important distinction). There is a 'triple agenda' – in the United States, Japan and Europe. But, despite the apparent globalness of events, the motivation for these changes is primarily domestic, even though issues of international competitiveness do feature in the debate (and the European process has a strong regional flavour). When it comes down to the legislative battles and the 'turf' wars over market share and regulatory control, the international perspective invariably becomes blurred by domestic struggles.

The United States is steadily reducing the barriers between financial sectors, even though Glass-Steagall (the 1930s laws separating commercial and investment banking) is taking a long time to die and the deregulation trend is constantly interrupted by financial crisis. Each crisis – such as the savings and loans (S&Ls) débâcle – either persuades deregulation advocates that the pace of change must accelerate or persuades conservatives that deregulation can hardly take place when financial firms are already losing money in their existing areas of business and expertise. Interest-rate deregulation has already been completed and the final barriers to inter-state banking are being removed. One barrier that is likely to remain in place is that preventing commercial enterprises from owning banks, at least without 'firewalls' preventing companies from having any degree of access to the financial support given to banks through lender of last resort and other facilities. The process also goes beyond the borders of the United States, most notably into Canada.

In *Japan* a similar rethink of the Glass-Steagall type of regulation (Article 65) is under way and, as in the United States, will ultimately encompass all sectors, including insurance. As in the United States in the 1970s, the Japanese reform process also includes interest-rate deregulation. Unique to the Japanese reform process is the possible revision of the various categories of bank that exist, with special privileges and roles assigned to different banks (city banks, trust banks, long-term credit banks, etc.).

In *Europe* the EC 1992 programme provides for a more rigorous timetable for regulatory change and is the sole example to date of regulatory structures being developed on a legal basis that extends beyond separate national states: i.e. on a supranational as well as a national basis (see Woolcock, et al., 1991). Within Europe, the United Kingdom has been radically reforming its own regulatory structure as London seeks to retain its position as a major international financial centre, and the dominant centre for Europe.

The international dimension and importance of these national and regional programmes emerges in a variety of often oblique ways. In the 1960s, the whole set of rules imposed and later disposed by the United States (Regulation Q, the Interest Equalization Tax, the Voluntary Foreign Credit Restraint Programme, the rules of the Office for Foreign Direct Investment) were all major forces encouraging US banks to switch activities to the fledgling euromarket. The Nixon shock of 15

August 1971 was certainly of global importance. In many respects the importance of these US measures reflected the importance of the United States and of the dollar as the hegemon and guarantor of the international financial system at the time, and the problems inherent in trying to retain that status.

Deregulation in the Japanese financial arena has tended to have less global importance except in so far as the world's desire to enter the Japanese market has increased as the significance and size of Japan itself has increased. More broadly, the power of the Japanese banks and securities houses has raised questions of the international competitiveness of Japanese and non-Japanese houses. For Japanese firms, international expansion has often been a route for avoiding domestic restrictions.

Finally, in Europe, the regulation agenda is now perhaps the most internationally significant of all three agendas: the European agenda contains all the ingredients of the debates elsewhere; all major players have to consider their future position in Europe; the European debate sees Anglo-Saxon systems coming up against universal banking structures; competition among stock exchanges is very keen; changes will be considerable in the retail sector, not being confined to global wholesale markets; and Europe provides the primary example of the development of supranational rules and arrangements. There are of course some efforts under way to develop a global framework for regulatory change in addition to these national agendas: the Uruguay Round's effort to develop an agreement on trade in services (GATS), especially in financial services, the work of the Organization for Economic Cooperation and Development to bring together OECD and non-OECD countries to discuss and analyse international financial markets and to develop the OECD codes of liberalization, the work of central banks through the Bank for International Settlements (BIS) and the work of IOSCO, the International Organization of Securities Commissions. These groups develop more cooperation among nations and regulators, even though they can only bring together national structures rather than develop a supranational or global rulebook.

A baker's dozen global issues

From these diverse agendas it is possible to extract thirteen issues which seem to have global and international importance. They are presented below in sub-groups, where the linkages are most obvious.

The regulatory revolution

Structure of market issues

(1) Removing sectoral barriers within the whole financial services industry. In the United States and Japan there are more formal barriers limiting access to different sectors than there are in Europe, where the barriers and sectoral divisions involve both legal and less formal segmentation. The alteration of these sectoral barriers are as important as the reduction of the geographical barriers, and, of course, where the approach to sectoral differences varies on a nation-by-nation basis, the differences run parallel to the national/geographical barriers. The scope of this sectoral interaction now goes well beyond banking and securities finance: it includes the whole insurance industry, the integration in Europe now labelled 'bancassurance' (see *International Financial Law Review*, 1991).

(2) Improving access to the more closed national markets, especially in Japan and the LDCs. This process is being pursued on both a bilateral basis (e.g. the yen/dollar talks) and a multilateral basis through the GATS (General Agreement on Trade in Services) part of the Uruguay Round of trade negotiations under the auspices of the GATT (General Agreement on Tariffs and Trade), which aims to bring services, especially financial services, into the multilateral trade negotiation framework. Access issues go to the heart of the integration process: improved access allows the market forces to bring different practices together and competitive forces to drive the process of harmonization and standardization. While access is denied, it is much easier for radically different systems to coexist and to retain their differences.

(3) Finance/commerce links. The relationship between the finance industry and its corporate clientele is of central importance to any debate over the efficiency and effectiveness of the financial system in the economy at large. Rules governing the ways in which finance and commerce mix (or are not allowed to mix) lie at the heart of many of the differences between nations' financial systems. How far can these different systems coexist in a more interdependent, integrated and globalized financial and economic system? It is in this area that the wider type of systemic frictions can arise, involving the competitiveness not just of financial firms but of companies more broadly and of economies. It is quite possible that this issue will be one of the more intractable issues over the coming decade, when the compromise solution will be to agree to differ.

Regulatory/supervisory issues

(4) Capital adequacy. By 1992 all banks engaging in international

activities will need to meet the common capital adequacy targets agreed under the auspices of the BIS, assuming that their own regulatory authorities are signatories to the BIS capital accord (i.e. all the Group of Ten countries, most of the OECD and in the future some of the developing nations). A similar exercise is being attempted for the securities business, typically less heavily capitalized, but progress has been very slow. The importance of the capital adequacy process to the end-of-geography story is that this represents the first attempt to develop a global rule or standard. It is not yet clear whether this process will prove a forerunner of further global rules or whether the problems in agreeing such a global standard will demonstrate the limits to global regulation in other areas. The capital adequacy story so far provides a good example of how cross-border agreements are in practice put into effect: although the Group of Ten countries had been discussing the process for some time, it was not until the US and the UK authorities took action on a bilateral basis to impose minimum ratios that the process was taken up by the Group of Ten and the EC. In this instance, the strong communality of purpose between the two English-speaking nations made their geographical separation across the Atlantic Ocean less of a barrier than the narrow passage of water separating the United Kingdom from the continent of Europe.

(5) Coordination of regulatory and supervisory authorities worldwide and within countries. From the early 1970s, banking supervisors began a long process of international coordination. This process continues, and efforts are under way to try to extend the process across the financial services industry, including regulators of stock markets, exchange managements and regulators of the insurance industry. The capital adequacy process came out of this, but goes wider. The record in the banking sector does not give a clear answer as to the future of the coordination. Although banking has shown a lead, the challenge is far greater in other areas as a result of much greater fragmentation. The banking process has already taken twenty years to be put together. Crises such as that of the Bank of Credit and Commerce International (BCCI) show where weaknesses still exist, even if fraud always has a good chance of beating the system.

Stock market issues

(6) Restructuring stock exchanges around new technologies. The whole format of stock market trading is being transformed by computerization. How exchanges, long structured around their trading floors, cope

23

with this change to computer trading is of course one of the most lively end-of-geography issues. Just where is the market when it exists in the computer system? Who regulates a market when its geographical co-ordinates can no longer be pinned down easily?

(7) Regulation of derivatives (the financial products such as futures and options that build on the basic cash markets). It is in the derivative markets that the greatest challenge is being made to traditional market locations, a classic end-of-geography challenge. Products once traded in one location can now be traded elsewhere. An investor can invest in the New York stock market by buying a product in Chicago. This presents regulators with a host of turf problems, including the question as to whether a futures product based on a market index is a stock product (to be regulated by the stock market regulator) or a futures product (to be regulated by a futures regulator). Clearly it is both, but a way has to be found to define the regulator responsibility. The exchanges are also attempting to preserve their independence while, at the same time, derivatives and other changes (e.g. in Europe) are forcing them to interrelate to a high degree.

Protecting the consumer

(8) Protecting the consumer. The global story is far from confined to the wholesale markets. Protecting the consumer is becoming a critical issue in financial regulation. As is discussed in more detail in Chapter 6, globalization has more relevance to retail markets than might appear at first glance. While many grey areas will exist, it is clear that regulators will tend to develop rules that adopt a different attitude to the consumer as opposed to the professional user of financial services. The problem may well lie in deciding just how far the consumer has to be protected: over-protection can be costly to the financial system, to the public purse and to the efficient workings of the economy itself.

(9) Deposit insurance. This issue could also be grouped with capital adequacy, given that it has a similar purpose in protecting the soundness of the system. However, in the policymaking arena it clearly is a major consumer issue, shown by the number of failed banks in the United States, the cost to the public purse, and the way in which the failure of BCCI in the United Kingdom and elsewhere hit consumers (who were not so well covered as in the United States). The EC is still considering whether deposit insurance should be dealt with via a directive coordinating insurance levels and conditions throughout the EC. In practice it may be expected that deposit insurance levels will have to converge. The main

debate may hinge on which government pays the insurance: the home or the host (i.e. the authority presiding over where the deposit was made, and marketed, or the authority that gave the licence to accept deposits in the first place). However this is resolved, it will be increasingly difficult to draw a firm line between home and host authorities, being geographical concepts which our thesis should undermine.

Operational and accounting questions

(10) International accounting standards. If money is truly defined by regulation it is the accounting profession that turns those legal definitions into dollars and cents. Accounting standards and practices differ widely across countries. Efforts to standardize such items as capital will not work in the long run if standardization of accounting is not vigorously pursued.

(11) Clearance and settlements. Like accounting, this issue rarely emerges in the public debate, but it is critical when dealing with detail and covers a wide range of problems. Following initial recommendations from the industry, harnessed by the Group of Thirty, a series of recommendations are being put into place. This effort is primarily confined to the wholesale market, although within the EC the progress towards a truly transparent single market depends on the improvement in interactiveness of retail payments systems across existing borders.

Information handling

(12) Money laundering and secrecy. Inspired by a global desire to control the drugs trade, a major global effort is being made to 'clean up' the world's financial system, to enable illegal monies to be traced. The BCCI example is a vivid reminder of the globalness of this problem and of how far we have in fact moved towards the end of geography. The intensity of this effort has even gone so far as to penetrate the secret world of Swiss banking, an achievement long thought impossible by those in pursuit of unpaid taxes and dictators' booty.

(13) Data protection issues. The explosion of technology has given rise to new legislation to protect the privacy of the individual and to regulate the storage and use of information. Computerization has rapidly expanded the scope for the manipulation of such data and for its cross-border transmission. Setting acceptable standards for such activities is a major task.

System coexistence and friction

In the final chapter of this paper we attempt to draw up a matrix of priorities on all these issues. Here it is enough to make a few comments. One of the most challenging issues in the end-of-geography sense is the question of systemic friction, a problem that results from the variety of sectoral barriers within countries' financial systems and the differences in terms of the cross-ownership between finance and commerce. In addition, the tasks of protecting the consumer in a globalized, innovating market and coordinating the multiple regulatory and supervisory authorities rank alongside these systemic friction issues in importance and difficulty. Perhaps all the other issues could conceivably be solved through painstaking negotiation, attention to detail and clarification of new responsibilities as the market changes. But separation of powers and cross-ownership strike close to the heart of the differences between, say, German universal banking, with integrated financial services (*allfinanz*), and the US structure, affecting not just the financial sector but the whole role of capital in these economies. Both systems are deeply ingrained in the national brand of capitalism, indeed in recent economic history.

Can these different systems coexist? The pressure is for the systems to move slowly towards a common structure. The separation of sectors is being eroded, mainly because of the trend towards securitization. Keeping the sectors separate, by law, is becoming more and more difficult. The barriers *are* falling. Ownership issues are moving more slowly.

The erosion of sectoral barriers suggests that the world is moving towards German-style universal banking, but this conclusion is likely to mislead if that is to suggest that the German system will prevail in its entirety. German universality has two distinct characteristics: close ownership links between commerce and banks; and universality in terms of what a bank can do. This system has resulted in a very lop-sided financial system, in which banking has dominated the securities business. The record of the German economy to date has not seemed to suffer from this characteristic, and the close bank/client relationship has its attractions. In contrast, often has been the time in the United Kingdom when either the banks or the stock markets have been called to account for their fairweather approach to clients. And often enough have US companies bemoaned the pressure of satisfying the stock market every quarter with good earnings, when the company would much rather be investing for the future but dare not do so for fear of takeover, or the like. Yet can we expect a shift to the German system, where the stock market has been pathetically small, if the shift towards securitization is one of the fundamental trends driving the changing financial services industry?

In practice, the German system is changing. The forces of securitization should mean an increasing role for the stock market and, in Europe, a development of other markets, such as European commercial paper markets. German financial firms will continue to be universal in the *allfinanz* sense, but there is every sign of continued specialization within the firm. Where does this leave the close relationship with the client? Should the client expect a coordinated service from all parts of the bank, or should the different parts be able to act independently, advise investment clients to sell the shares of the company when the bank is a major lender, etc? This aspect is closely influenced by the second aspect of the German universal system, the links between finance and industry. As the banking market becomes more open and competitive, it would seem that companies are going to be offered more and more finely priced specialist services. If big companies can tap open markets for credit (disintermediating the banks), then the *hausbank* relationship may wither on the vine. Relationship banking may still make a comeback, but in a specialist way. If the relationship becomes specialist, even within a single financial conglomerate, does the ownership link help or does it become a hindrance?

Of course the friction will be manifested not so much by conflict between systems as by competition among the firms themselves and within firms. Integration will depend on how far the domestic banks can defend their turf. To a great extent the market will decide the future structure of the global financial services industry.

Regulation redefines the macro role of money

Regulations affect the provision of credit and offer new opportunities to savers. Obviously all these changes have a direct impact on the conduct of monetary policy. The monetary authorities are also engaged in a constant struggle to balance the aims of monetary policy with the aims of prudential regulation (albeit not necessarily always acting in opposing directions).

In an open financial system it becomes increasingly difficult to police the system through direct controls; supervision and prudential regulation become harder to run, and it may be argued that an increasing burden falls upon the broader monetary policy. United Kingdom experience shows how financial liberalization and deregulation has made it harder to achieve monetary policy targets and aims, as the practices of the market change and as the interpretation and measurement of monetary variables has become more difficult (another example of Goodhart's Law, which states that as soon as a monetary aggregate is targeted it changes its behaviour). Cause and effect are all tied into each other.

The development and widening usage of new financial products also alters the running of monetary policy. In the retail sector, the 1980s have seen a widening use of plastic credit and the electronic provision of financial services. At the wholesale end, the introduction of new products and markets presents the regulators with major headaches in terms of defining what should be permitted, where to draw the line between innovation as a force for beneficial change and adaptation and innovation as a dangerous destabilizing force. Money and credit appear in many new guises.

4

THE EUROMARKET STORY: TOWARDS GLOBAL BANKING

The origins of the eurocurrency markets go back to the early postwar years, starting with Chinese dollar deposits being placed in a Soviet-owned bank in France in 1949, and Soviet dollar deposits being placed in the same bank almost a decade later; the telex answerback code of this bank just happened to be EUROBANK. These communist dollar holdings were looking for a safe haven in case the US authorities should attempt to block them. So began the process that was to see billions of dollars and other hard currencies deposited and lent outside the domestic capital markets of the world's major economies.

Global credentials

The euromarket (not, of course, to be confused with that other euro-market, the EEC, which started at about the same time) and its constituent parts – the euro-deposit market, the euro-syndicated credit market, the eurobond market and the FX market – together still provide the best examples of global financial markets. The global credentials of these markets are several: there are few restrictions on entry; any country's bank can set up in the euromarket, taking international deposits and lending those funds internationally; anyone can place money on deposit, subject to any existing exchange controls at home; the market has no formal geographical base or national home, apart from its euro-name and the prominence of London as a major centre of this global activity, which provides little connection with the United Kingdom as such. Symbolic of the geographical centre of this global activity was the acronym LIBOR

(London Inter-Bank Offered Rate), being the benchmark interest rate, its 11 a.m. fix every day being the reference rate for almost all eurocurrency loans.

The market was, of course, primarily offshore rather than truly global at the beginning, and would appear firmly in the centre of the diagram in Figure 1 (Chapter 1). The euromarket had strong links to national financial markets, although barriers around the national markets resulted in pricing differentials between domestic and offshore money. The market was essentially developed to avoid geography or national control: from the original motivation of the early communist depositors to avoid other nations' controls through to the stimulus given by the various restrictions placed by the US regulators on US banks' domestic activities and efforts to shore up the US balance of payments. Although the late 1950s and 1960s was a period of increasing international economic interdependence, it was also the period of fixed exchange rates held together by exchange controls and restrictions, despite the IMF's declared intent to eliminate such restrictions.

Of course, the developments were not wholly new to the world. Depositing money offshore, in foreign bank accounts, has a much longer history than the euromarket: Swiss banks have been taking foreigners' deposits for years, as indeed were the Italian banks in the fourteenth century. To round out the euromarket concept (as opposed to the fiduciary role played by Swiss banks, which involves taking clients' deposits and placing them elsewhere), there had to be a form of lending to match the new offshore deposit-placing.

Early euro-borrowers
In the earliest days the demand for eurocurrency loans came as a result of an increase in activities in Europe by US multinationals. One of the first borrowers of eurodollars was IBM Europe. Although this was in the days of fixed exchange rates and thus limited FX risk, lending dollars to a company in Europe might have been considered problematic if that company had no clear stream of dollar earnings or access to dollars for repayment. IBM Europe, however, was seen as ultimately having access to dollars through its parent, and thus lending dollars to IBM did not seem to pose any 'geographical' mismatch problem (in this case identifying the company and the currency as one). Eventually, as the depth of the deposit market in various currencies grew and the lending market developed, that perceived need to link borrower nationality and currency

disappeared. IBM Europe itself has proved to be an interesting example of a company seeking to give itself a different geographical identity, being as European as American.

At this initial stage the currency question was more one of access to the right currency for repayment, just as the issue of lender of last resort was related to access to liquidity. In the 1970s, of course, choice of currency took on a whole new dimension under the regime of floating exchange rates. As access to different currencies became freer, its price varied more widely. Those companies who did not fully appreciate the risks they were running soon discovered the potential costs if they were not hedged. For example, a number of UK companies that borrowed low-interest Swiss francs in the mid-1970s were very badly burnt, when the effective cost of those loans, translated into sterling terms, soared to 50% on an annualized basis when sterling fell against the Swiss franc. Even today, with far more sophisticated hedging vehicles available to companies and to all financial houses, big losses are still made (and presumably profits, though not so well publicized) by currency mismatching with respect to assets, liabilities, and income and payment streams.

A push to international banking

From an organizational point of view the euromarket was important in giving international banking a major push and *raison d'être*. All this activity added to the traditional international activities of banks, whether in the field of international trade finance or in adding a new dimension to the extensive branch networks which many banks, especially US banks, had begun to develop. Correspondent banking, where banks provide services to other banks across the globe, was facilitated by the euromarket growth. For career-minded bankers, international banking became the place to be, as opposed to domestic retail banking, which had long been the primary earner for most banks. The growth of international business added to the value of banks' overseas branches and representative networks. Most branches have a dual function: operating in the domestic market, taking local deposits and on-lending locally (where the licence permitted), and at the same time servicing multinational corporate customers in international trade finance and local finance and payments services. The globalness of such a service to, say, a multinational would be both in offering a service in foreign markets and in providing international services. The market was by no means integrated or global in the sense that we have defined global for our purposes here. The aim of the bank would be to provide the customer with the service which the customer would expect in a global integrated market: i.e. with the means of overcoming the barriers that did exist. The lack of integration would be reflected in the differential cost of money in each market, and the bank's fee and earnings would be, in effect, for providing a global service where a global market did not exist.

For the banks, further connections between domestic business and international business developed as host governments began to look to foreign banks with a local presence to provide international support, especially in the form of term loans (often balance-of-payments loans). That international lending aspect was to increase very significantly the country risk that banks with a large international network would take on (whereas a branch or subsidiary would have only its capital at risk, with the rest of the local book being financed domestically).

Of course what we can observe here is the development of global networks as links between markets develop even where barriers still exist. A global network in effect seeks to offer a global service but does not depend on integration of markets. Advancing technology is offering more ways of developing global networks in addition to the base of a physical presence in each market. Correspondent banking is a classic networking business. Networking – one of the new 'buzzwords' of the international scene – via computers adds a new layer to the more traditional networking through personal and institutional relationships and agreements.

In several respects national aspects have continued to shape the market. Most of the participant banks can be easily identified as national banks, whether US, British, Swiss, French, German, Arab or Japanese. Their international roles did vary significantly according to their own national characteristics: German banks lent more heavily to Eastern Europe, whereas US banks played a dominant role in Latin America; Japanese banks found the interbank deposit premium rose against them, en bloc, when the future of the Japanese economy was seen to be in serious jeopardy following the first oil-price hike. There was still a tendency for business to be linked to the servicing of national corporate customers. Syndication responsibilities were often organized along nationality lines, with, say, a Japanese bank as a lead manager for Japanese banks, a German bank for German participants, and so on, although of course syndication was also organized by financial centres (another geographical cut of the cake).

The consortia banks were more multinational by way of their share-holdings, but eventually the question of who was responsible, jointly and severally, was sorted out and allocated on a national basis. The demise of the consortia came either when the national owners became concerned as to the exposures the consortia were taking on their behalf or when the international departments of the shareholder banks found themselves in competition with their own part-owned consortia subsidiary. The majority of the participants, however, were clearly national banks. None the less, geography and nationality could be ignored, most obviously with banks specializing in the trading of currencies other than their national currency (although, again, most banks would have a natural deposit base in their domestic currency and would be seen as potential market leaders in the eurosector of that currency).

In short, the euromarket offered a global pooling of funds which could be tapped by borrowers from anywhere (as long as their own domestic authorities permitted the borrowing of foreign currencies) and where depositors could place their monies (again subject to national restrictions). As the international business of multinationals increased, and as international trade boomed, there was an increasing amount of money which was earned outside domestic markets and which could therefore be put to work outside those confines. The importance of the offshore euromarket grew relative to the domestic banking markets, even though the fears that domestic monetary policies would be distorted by a domin-ant euromarket were to be unfulfilled. The euromarket became the con-necting rod between separate money markets as well as an additional marketplace in its own right, but still dependent on the existence of the trading national entities.

Although the euromarket had its origins in the early postwar years, its activities really came to life and to the forefront of international economic activity in the early 1970s, as a result of the twin events of the flotation of exchange rates (1971) and the recycling task which started with the first oil crisis (1973). No discussion of the markets can be complete without a separate look at both phenomena.

Floating exchange rates and the global FX market

August 1971 was clearly one of the most important watersheds of post-war economic history. The advent of floating exchange rates was a critical factor in creating the end-of-geography condition, and meant three things: (1) the growth in the FX market, perhaps the best example of a global financial market we have seen; (2) a boom in international capital flows following the liberalization of capital controls after the demise of the fixed-rate, controlled system; and (3) the end of dollar hegemony, and the emergence of new international economic and currency alliances. As a result of these changes we now have an international financial system which is often seen as being run by the global investor, where global portfolio preferences determine the fate of currencies rather than some safer world where somehow exchange rates are determined by observable flows of trade in goods and services. The world's money managers are seen to exercise great global power, with the capital account determining the current account, rather than the other way round.

What makes the FX market peculiarly global? Obviously it has to be called international, since all exchange rates involve different countries. Its globalness comes from a number of features. First, all currencies are involved (to a greater or lesser degree) so that the complex web of different exchange rates (a multilateral set of relationships) covers the globe. Second, an exchange rate is a globally understood concept and a currency is a globally understood and tradable product or commodity. Third, there are no barriers to entry to the FX market, except those imposed behind exchange controls. And, finally, all international financial transactions and transfers will pass through the FX market or will lead to an FX transaction.

The globalness of the FX market means that it has no special geographical home, although practitioners do tend to congregate in certain locations, and every currency certainly has a geographical and national home (see Bank of England, 1989, for data on who trades what currencies and where). All this is done through computer networks and over the telephone. Physical contact, beyond the dealing rooms of the players, is hardly necessary. An FX book can be instantly transferred anywhere on the globe: banks' global positions are transferred around the clock, though time-zones still impose certain geographical restrictions on the market. The information needed to analyse currencies is easily transmitted across the screens. Of course, local understanding of local economies is important to the market's understanding of the factors behind each currency, but it is much easier to analyse currencies from afar than, say, companies.

Of course the FX market depends upon the existence of separate national currencies: the ultimate global integrated world of a single currency would mean no FX market. The very idea of a currency embodies the idea of the separate nation, representing therefore the idea of political and indeed economic geography. Giving up the national currency is seen as the abandonment of sovereignty. But this does not detract from the integrated nature of the market worldwide. It is the increasing integration and interconnection of market participants that give the market its global nature. Different currencies play different roles in this global FX market. The major currencies play a role as investment currencies, being bought and sold by many who have no underlying trade with the country. An internationalized currency is a globalized currency. Other currencies are traded more by those with reasons to be involved with the country. Each restriction of course offers arbitrage opportunities and risk/reward opportunities. Currency fluctuations result from the different characteristics of each currency and the issuing country.

Recycling and the global loan market

On 6 October 1973, an event occurred that was to transform the euromarket and the world economy for the next twenty years. In particular this event would have a special effect upon the developing world. The Yom Kippur war triggered the first oil crisis, led to the quadrupling of the price of oil and a massive shift of income from oil consumers to oil producers.

The oil crisis and the ensuing recycling drama had a number of important influences on our story. Most dramatically, recycling presented the by-now reasonably confident euromarket with its first major task and first major test: a massive international payment dislocation to be intermediated by the market. This is not the place to revisit the whole episode, but for the first six years at least the market appeared to acquit itself well, recycling oil surpluses to oil importers, offering oil producers a safe home for their funds and preventing immediate payments dislocation for the oil consumers. Different economies chose different ways of coping with the problem: not all decided to finance their way through the 1970s, but the market was there if need be.

In this pre-securitization decade the recycling was carried out by banks making loans (held on their own balance sheets) rather than by investment banks placing bonds in the market. Why? On the asset (loan) side, many of the borrowers were relatively new entities: country risk analysts had to be hired by the banks to assess the new borrowers, to approve these new loan assets. Placing LDC assets with the legendary Belgian dentists and other eurobond purchasers would have been much more difficult (not to mention the fact that the prewar bond markets had also been damaged by defaults on Latin American bonds). On the liability (deposit) side, euromarket banks were a neutral place to deposit funds. Banks were eager to do the business and had the ability to compete for the job.

The recycling era brought the developing world into the limelight of the international financial markets in a major way, including many newly independent nations. Of course this was not the first time that Latin American nations had tapped the international capital markets: the last episode had also ended in tears, but all that was a long time ago. LDCs became not only borrowers (and thus important banking clients) but depositors too. Further business began to be developed in advising economies how to invest their funds and, after a while, how to reschedule their debts.

Recycling required innovation, albeit nothing like as complex as the innovation boom of the securities markets of the 1980s. But the market had two tasks on its hands at this time: how to recycle and how to deal with floating interest rates and floating exchange rates. In the event, the relatively simple floating-rate rollover loan was devised, with large deals being syndicated among groups of banks. The borrower took the long-term interest risk, while all the bank had to do was fund the shorter-term rollover periods. Of course, when the balloon went up and the 'double-whammy' of higher interest rates and lower commodity prices put paid to the economic prospects of many countries, the risk implicitly fell back to the banks in the form of bad debts.

This boom in activity gave us a major international credit market and indeed a global market. While syndication efforts took place often in major financial centres, and borrowers had roadshows around the globe, the market was extremely well interconnected. Fees and spreads were well known, even though this information did not legally have to be published everywhere. The desire for publicity, to attract new business, ensured that deals *were* published, although the fees and spreads were obtainable only from market knowledge and related closely to other factors, such as the type of deal. Pricing of credits became a matter of pride and status for the borrower, as in all markets.

This activity was, however, largely unregulated except that every participating bank was regulated and supervised in its turn. Concerns as to where this build-up in LDC debt was heading were often expressed, but, by the time the position became untenable, the damage was done. Not all the large debtors hit the rocks: the fourth largest LDC debtor is now a creditor (South Korea).

There has been a major fallout from this episode: many banks have pulled back from international lending, especially to LDCs. Yet trade finance continues, and the eagerness to open up LDC financial markets, as negotiated under the Uruguay Round, indicates the desire to service these underdeveloped markets. At the same time, the richer LDCs are in no hurry to integrate: Korea and Taiwan, for example, are not particularly keen to open up fully or deregulate their financial markets.

The crisis also seriously weakened American banks, who until then had led the global banking charge. As the LDC debt crisis broke, so world attention was being grabbed by the large surpluses being accumulated by Japan. A new global imbalance was emerging. This time it was the turn of the securities markets and a boom in direct and portfolio investments. And, instead of unknown LDCs having to tap bank credit, there was a ready supply of US government paper available for anyone with surplus funds.

Early end-of-geography challenges

The euromarket presented a number of end-of-geography challenges to the authorities. It was soon clear to the financial authorities that its location had to be identified more precisely, in order to define who was responsible for its actions. The authorities had four main areas of concern, covering issues of monetary policy, lender-of-last-resort facilities, supervision and settlements. All these issues are good examples of end-of-geography challenges to the existing regulatory structures.

The first concern was that these pools of offshore monies might constitute a challenge to monetary policy as exercised by national governments, and that the credit-creating potential of eurobanks posed an inflationary threat. Over time these concerns were assuaged; central banks were still, after all, the only issuers of currency, although analytical and reporting techniques had to be refined to account for the euromarket activities of banks. The euromarket offered cheaper funds from banks not restricted by reserve requirements, and a flexibility unhampered by exchange controls or interest-rate ceilings. What emerged were two-tier markets: eurodollar rates and domestic dollar rates, eurosterling rates and domestic sterling rates (where there were exchange controls). On the whole, the underlying interest rates continued to be determined by national monetary policy: the eurorates were a function of the national rates.

The second challenge to public policy focused on the operation of the lender of last resort vis-à-vis banks operating in the euromarket (including such new entities as the multinationally owned consortium banks). Not only was there the question of who owned what to be clarified; if lender of last resort support had to be provided, which central bank would be responsible for, say, providing dollars to a foreign bank in the United States, or providing European currency to a US bank in Europe? This currency issue was of particular importance at a time of exchange controls and of segmenting domestic and offshore money markets.

The third challenge, over supervision, was eventually addressed by bank supervisors in the early 1970s. From this exercise has emerged the most important work in terms of developing a form of global regulation, from the early agreements on supervisory responsibilities in banking through to the more recent capital adequacy accords and the efforts to extend the net to cover supervision of other financial services activities.

The final challenge related to the more mundane issue of global settlements in the international market (a question raised most dramatically in 1974 by the failure of the small German private bank Bankhaus I.D. Herstatt, even though its failure was related to foreign exchange-rate speculation losses obtained in the brave new world of floating exchange rates). The settlements issue has become of critical importance today in the securities industry and is now the focus of intense efforts to develop a more watertight system to prevent any major accident in the settlements system involving billions of interconnected payments. For example, the so-called 'meltdown' that threatened at the time of the 1987 stock-market crash was a result more of the sheer pressure on settlements and the trading system than of the size of the crash itself.

The euromarket story provides a good example of a global market: the FX market. The euromarket developed as an offshore market, not a global market according to the definitions set out in Chapter 1, but none the less the world's largest international loan market. The 'country risk' losses that emerged were a classic example of geographical risks at work. But, as exchange controls have reduced the barriers between this offshore market and the domestic markets, the market has come closer to the global, integral concept. The euromarket stimulated the first attempt to develop global rules, through the effort of the banking supervisors meeting in Basle. The question of how far this process is likely to continue in other sectors of the financial services industry leads to consideration of the globalization of the securities market in the 1980s.

5

SECURITIES MARKETS: BIG BANGS ACROSS THE GLOBE

If the 1970s saw the advent of the first big global banking markets, the 1980s was the decade of the global securities market boom, driven both by the trend towards securitization of finance and by increased activity by securities firms across a larger number of markets worldwide. More firms were granted access to stock exchanges in other countries, enabling them to trade stocks and government bonds. The most obvious examples of this form of global expansion were the Big Bang in the United Kingdom in 1986, and the increased presence of foreign securities firms on the Tokyo Stock Exchange, itself becoming a more internationally important exchange as the Japanese economy boomed and as Japan became the world's largest capital exporter. The price of a seat on the Tokyo exchange rivalled even the price of membership of a Tokyo golf club. (The long-term value of both will be seen more clearly in the 1990s.)

The trend towards securitization saw more business being directed towards the securities industry and, while the boom lasted, more banks entering the business, often by purchasing securities firms. But, as we shall see, globalization means far more than more firms setting up shop in more locations across the globe. Furthermore, because the structure and nature of national securities markets and their regulation tend to differ more, country by country, than do banking structures, the increase in global securities markets presents a more complex picture than did the globalization of banking markets in the 1970s.

Securitization and globalization

Securitization means the making of an open market in financial assets; globalization is encouraged by that openness. Open markets provide for much wider and deeper sets of relationships between buyer and seller, between borrower and investor, than do closed systems based on borrower and depositor relations with individual institutions, typified by on-balance-sheet banking (even though much of banking requires a market to be developed, such as in the syndication or even the private placement of deals). But the greater the quatity of the trading business carried out by the market, the better the pricing should be and the more transparent the deals transacted. The role of the securities intermediary becomes one of trading the instrument as opposed to taking the full credit risk, by placing the asset with the market rather than on the securities firm's own balance sheet. This greater openness allows more players to be involved in the deals and encourages more open competition outside the traditional clubs and institutions.

Of course, securitization presents a direct challenge to banking, and restructures the whole system of financial intermediation. While the securities markets were booming in the 1980s, the international banking business was retrenching after its previous excesses, and banking continues to be under considerable pressure, not least as banks seek to build stronger capital bases to meet the new capital adequacy requirements. But the early 1990s are also seeing the securities business recovering from its excesses: perhaps the 1990s will be characterized by a boom in insurance business worldwide, as well as the broader restructuring of the financial services industry across the board.

Borrowers and investors

Capital markets (as distinct from transaction-related financial services) exist to provide those needing capital with that capital, and investors with investment opportunities. The securities firms generally play the intermediary role between borrower and investor, as brokers and traders rather than as principals (unlike banks). Although the financial firms often seem to call the shots in day-to-day activities, ultimately their very existence depends upon being able to meet the needs of borrowers and investors. As a result, any important trend in the market, such as globalization or securitization, can be traced back to changes in the needs, attitudes and behaviour of borrowers and/or investors. For example, the structure of international banking in the 1970s was shaped by the sudden need of many LDCs for finance, and the need of the countries of OPEC (Organization of Petroleum Exporting Countries) for investment opportunities. The need of investors and borrowers to cope with floating exchange rates after 1971 led to the growth of the FX and international money markets. The quality of the market will be influenced by the quality of the service provided by the intermediary, but it is the changing investment and funding needs that instigate the process. No business transactions, no intermediary.*

Wider choices
From the point of the view of those raising capital, securitization is attractive if it provides better access to sources of longer-term capital than that offered by bank credit. By 'better', the borrower has in mind the amount of finance available, the price and the tenor/maturity of that finance, and the reliability of the financial support. The more that the securities markets develop, the more that the market will offer good pricing, reliability of support and the required volumes of finance. Globalization helps to widen the range in terms of sources of finance. In so far as globalization improves competition among those providing the funds or among those offering a home for savers' funds, the user of that financial service should be able to expect better pricing. In many respects globalization represents the breaking up of existing cartels, finance clubs and markets, which may not have offered the borrower the best price (though closed systems also have their advantages). It is likely that, as different financial systems are forced to coexist together, the more open, market-style intermediary systems will begin to triumph over the closed systems. This is of course a key end-of-geography issue.

Access to a global securities market carries a cost for the borrower. For example, a firm may feel restricted by the limited circle of banks which may offer credit, and may welcome the chance to raise monies from elsewhere, such as the open securities market. But if that market suddenly drops the stock price, for reasons wholly unrelated to the firm but due to some wider shift in portfolio preference, the firm is the first to call foul. In a bull market, the equity market is everyone's friend: in a bear market, the equity market seems to underestimate everyone's pros-

---

*The term intermediary is used here to describe the role of the securities firm, even though the term disintermediation is also used to describe the move to eliminate the middleman role played by the bank, when a borrower is able to access funds directly in the marketplace, albeit using a securities firm as a middleman.

pects and wipes millions off the value of companies overnight. Suddenly there is nostalgia for the friendly embrace of the staid, but reliable and, perhaps more to the point, locked-in, house bank (which faces the choice between rescheduling the debt or having a bad loan). Of course, banks may also seem to act as fair-weather friends, one minute plying the client with loans, the next switching to conditions popularized recently as 'credit crunch'. The relevant point, however, is that, aside from the question of cyclical reliability of lender or stock market shareholder, securitization offers the borrower a wider choice of funding, and globalization (in banking or securities activities) widens the dimension still further. To a degree, how attractive the breadth of choice proves to be will have much to do with how far the companies themselves widen the scope of their business: the more international the business, the wider known will be the company to potential investors, and thus the more chance the firm should have to ensure that it can keep the global stock markets informed about the company's prospects.

Global investor diversification

None of this would take place, however, unless investors were also broadening their horizons, globally and internationally. For the investor, securitization and globalization offer more opportunities, deeper markets, more choice of borrower, more market liquidity. Particularly important in recent years has been the greater attention given to international risk diversification as a key factor in determining the portfolio preference of investors. Diversification has been encouraged both by regulations that have allowed a wider range of risks to be taken on and by regulations that have actively sought to encourage diversification. In addition, the evidence is that such international diversification has raised the return on investments, usually (though not always) a key determinant of investment strategies (see Davis, 1991).

A classic example of recent years has been the impact of the US ERISA legislation (Employees Retirement Investment Act), which effectively ruled that US pension funds should adopt diversification as a major risk-avoidance strategy, rather than the previous strategy of limiting investments to strictly defined rated instruments. Elsewhere, the relaxation of exchange controls has resulted in portfolio changes as institutions have steadily increased the overseas content of their portfolios. Such international diversification was often possible for the private investor able to keep monies abroad, but, for investment institutions (pension funds and insurance companies), investments have to conform to regulatory requirements. At the same time, however, although exchange controls have been lifted, many countries still require the institutions to hedge the bulk of their long-term liabilities by currency, effectively meaning that the funds have to have a majority of their assets in local currency investments to match their largely local currency liabilities. Realistically this will change only as such restrictions are removed, and only as the investment funds themselves begin to build international liabilities, a tendency that is likely to be seen in Europe.

Risk diversification increases the demand for a wider range of instruments and opportunities: a wider group of currencies, companies and countries in the portfolio, more markets (viz. greater interest in the emerging stock markets) and more innovative instruments to manage risk. Investment strategies that identify themes (e.g., investing in oil company stocks) need an adequate supply of investment opportunities to provide for diversification within the theme. The risk always remains that a theme strategy goes badly wrong: to avoid this there should be investment across a wide range of themes. This global and sectoral/thematic diversification approach also means that more investors will tend to buy a company's stock not because they know the company well but because they like the sector or the market or country that the company is in. The company, therefore, finds that its access to monies depends on how it is perceived as part of the wider portfolio strategies of the investors. Hence the securities markets can prove, on occasion, to be less friendly than the local banking market.

The global investment approach has already become well established in the currency and bond markets. Currencies and government bonds are well understood as investment instruments across the globe, at least for the wholesale investor. Companies, on the other hand, exhibit many more individual characteristics (countries and currencies do too, but we believe we can examine them quite well in a common framework, and there are far more individual companies than there are currencies). The global investor therefore buys collections of a market's stocks (indices). Stock-picking – identifying companies where there is some additional value – becomes a specialist activity rather than the core business of the global investor fund manager.

In short, for the professional investor, the end of geography is here to a great degree. As foreign exchange controls have been removed, monies can be easily invested in all major currencies. Investment in most stock markets can be carried out, and on a 24-hour basis, with more companies trading on more exchanges. There are restrictions still on investing in some of the stock markets that are emerging in developing countries, usually restricting the extent of foreign ownership or restricting the intermediary role to local firms. Country funds have been developed to provide the foreign investor with the vehicle for investing where such restrictions still exist. Perhaps most powerfully, capital markets have been effectively integrated through the swap market, allowing borrowers to obtain better terms from distant markets even where their name is less well known. Ultimately, there are few borders or barriers that cannot be overcome, albeit at a price.

For the retail (often smaller) investor, globalization effectively brings more investment opportunities closer. In practice, the retail investor benefits at arm's length, with the funds being invested by pension funds and the investment institutions (notably the insurance companies) on the smaller investor's behalf. None the less, as laws are relaxed, selling international investment products to the less-sophisticated investor is becoming more possible, posing the regulator and the markets (as self-regulators) with the challenge to ensure that the investor is not drawn too easily into unfamiliar territory, especially the smaller retail investor, who may not fully appreciate the risks or legal status of the investments.

Three important angles with respect to the securities industry provide a focus for discussing the end-of-geography challenge, namely the competition between stock exchanges, the impact of derivative markets, and the implications of the move from the old trading floors to the computer screens and networks.

The London Stock Exchange: the world's most global stock market?
Changes at the London Stock Exchange indicate the possible direction of the global stock market. Few exchanges are as international in scope or purpose as London, with the possible exception of Amsterdam. Some 553 foreign companies are listed on the exchange, more than on any other single market. But, because of the large number of UK stocks listed, this is only 21% of the companies listed in London, compared with much higher ratios of foreign to total stocks in Frankfurt, Paris, Amsterdam and Zurich. The US markets and Tokyo have relatively few foreign stock listings (see Table 1). At present, Tokyo is still primarily a market in Japanese company stocks and New York in US stocks.

In 1990, turnover in London of foreign equities exceeded that of domestic stocks for the first time, primarily a result of the growth of

Table 1 Number of companies listed as at the end of 1990

	Domestic	Foreign	Foreign as % of total	Total
Amsterdam	260	238	47.8	498
London	2,006	553	21.6	2559
Frankfurt	389	354	47.6	743
Paris	443	226	33.8	669
Zurich	182	240	35.9	422
Australia	1162	33	2.8	1195
Hong Kong	284	15	5.0	299
NASDAQ	3875	256	6.2	4131
NYSE	1678	96	5.4	1774
Tokyo	1627	125	7.1	1752
Toronto	1127	66	5.5	1193

Source: *Quality of Markets Quarterly Review*, London Stock Exchange, January–March 1991.

Table 2 Equity turnover on major exchanges, 1990, in £bn (sales only)

	Domestic	Foreign	Total	%*
London	157.1	147.8	304.9	12
Federation of German Exchanges	286.6	6.7	293.3	11
of which, Frankfurt	172.8	4.3	177.1	7
Paris	64.9	2.5	67.4	3
NYSE	n.a.	n.a.	748.5	29
NASDAQ	243.2	15.9	259.1	10
Tokyo	730.3	7.3	738.2	29

n.a. – not available, but author (Worthington) reports that NYSE foreign equity turnover was estimated at 25% of London's in 1st quarter 1990.
*Indicates the turnover of the exchange (domestic and foreign) as a proportion of the turnover of all exchanges.
Source: P.M. Worthington, *Bank of England Quarterly Bulletin*, May 1991.

SEAQI (the exchange's screen-based market for trading foreign equities). Clients dealing in foreign stocks are mainly professionals, and the size of transactions in foreign stocks is, on average, almost twice the size of domestic bargains. Each market's stock index still does not reflect the activity in foreign stocks: the indices compiled out of the top 30–100 shares in all cases still cover just the domestic stocks.

Although London is ahead of the game in terms of international trading, there has been an increase in cross-border trading of equities worldwide, averaging 35% growth in 1979–89 (according to Salomon Brothers data, see *Quality of Markets Quarterly Review*, July–September 1990), and in 1989 being the equivalent of 13.6% of trading in domestic stocks worldwide. SEAQI accounted for 46% of this activity in 1989. Table 2 reports more recent data on turnover in domestic and foreign stocks on all major exchanges, confirming the international dominance of London and the importance of international share-trading there.

The amount of trading in foreign stocks on any exchange obviously depends on a variety of factors, but perhaps most important is the willingness of the exchange to allow foreign-owned firms to trade on the exchange. Foreign players bring in a greater international interest in a wider range of stock, based on their own expertise and the needs of their clients. The growth of the business then depends on the development of sufficient depth to the market in those foreign stocks. Hence London has actively encouraged foreign participation as part of a strategy to become a truly international exchange, while Tokyo has protected its market from too many foreign players and has been content to see its size depend on domestic equity trading. Encouraging foreign business does require adaptation by the exchanges. As the New York Stock Exchange chairman, William Donaldson, put it, 'If this nation is to be the international marketplace for securities, we must recognize the obvious, that not all the quality companies in the world are US companies, nor are all US accounting standards and practices necessarily the only way of approaching disclosure.' (Speech to the National Press Club, 4 March 1991, quoted in *Quality of Markets Quarterly Review*, spring 1991.) This is a classic statement recognizing the end-of-geography challenge.

London is the market closest to losing its particular national flavour: the City, of course, has long been primarily an international centre, often laying itself open to the charge that its activities are too divorced from the needs of UK industry. In practice, the large UK companies will benefit from the international nature of the London market, and their own business often makes them international rather than purely domestic companies. The small companies will increasingly look to the different markets in London to service their needs. However, even this most internationally minded exchange is wary of losing its national base. This dilemma can be seen neatly in the changing attitude to the name of the exchange: in Big Bang days the market renamed itself the International Stock Exchange (previously simply the Stock Exchange). In 1991 it changed its name yet again, to the London Stock Exchange – who said anything about the end of geography?

'Vive la géographie'?

Going beyond London, the European debate among stock exchanges shows that not everyone favours the end of geography for stock markets. The end-of-geography approach, championed by London, is being contested by a *'vive la géographie'* approach of the French Bourse. The French strategy tries to preserve geography by aiming to ensure that all trades in French company stocks pass through the Paris Bourse.

This is geographical in two senses: first, it aims to preserve parochial control over the trading of domestic company stocks, rather than aiming to deal in a wider group of shares, in European or other companies (in direct contrast to London's increasing shift towards trading in non-UK stocks); second, it presupposes that in the future it will still be easy to identify French versus Italian versus British stocks, when companies themselves are becoming more European and/or global in an end-of-geography world. Of course, the strategy may well be a more feasible option if the Bourse feels it cannot compete on the international level. But in an end-of-geography world will it be realistic to try to confine trades in French stocks to one market if those companies could enjoy better conditions elsewhere, as a result of tapping a wider marketplace? Does this serve the interests of either the borrower or the investor, whether French, foreign or of mixed, uncertain parentage? Of course, for many small companies, who will be confined largely to domestic business themselves, there will be little interest in trading their stocks outside Paris. The main competitive issue at the European and more global level is the trading of the larger companies, especially as they themselves become more global or at least European.

It would be a mistake, as always, to assign a single approach to any one country. Although the French Bourse represents what I have termed a *'vive la géographie'* approach, the Paris-based futures and options market, the MATIF, is one of the most aggressive and internationally minded exchanges, linked up with Chicago through Globex (the global exchange network being set up by a number of exchanges) and actively competing with other futures exchanges. In practice the approach is different from the Paris Bourse because the futures business is a relatively new business and is very much shaped by globalization. Which brings us neatly to the question of the derivative markets.

Derivative markets

The term 'derivative business' effectively covers all trading outside the spot markets, including futures and options markets, swaps, and stock index options. Although futures have long existed in many markets (e.g. commodities), the 1980s saw a rapid increase in derivative markets and a plethora of innovations and financial packages. Almost any spot trade can be the base for a derivative market: it merely depends upon how much interest there is in the product, which itself determines how liquid the market is. Of course, derivative products can hardly be traded or developed without the primary cash markets being there. Indeed, at crisis times the problem has been how to trade the index if the spot (cash) market has stopped trading for technical reasons.

Regulatory structures and intense competition between exchanges has resulted in many apparent anomalies emerging. Trading in German Bund futures is dominated by the London International Financial Futures Exchange (LIFFE), where the first Bund futures contracts were traded; now the German exchanges are trying to win back business. There is no reason why, if the London market is more liquid, the Bund should not trade more heavily there, but clearly the German exchanges feel that their own national government debt should trade more heavily at home. In an end-of-geography world it does not matter where the Bund trades, or which national angle is important, if any. If all the trades were done on behalf of German investors by a British trader, itself a subsidiary of a French bank, whose market is it? What matters is that the exchanges, representing their member trading firms (an international, cosmopolitan crowd), want the trading to be done at their exchange, to earn the commissions for their member firms, and the ultimate buyers and sellers want the best price. It really matters little to German monetary policy where the Bund is traded.

Competition between the exchanges for derivative business is very intense in the United States, not least because Chicago had been the leader in all this innovation. A classic example is in the trading of the New York Stock Exchange index on the Chicago Board Options Exchange. The index option allows investors effectively to invest in the New York market without trading in New York. Who really regulates this trading? What happens if there is an interruption of information or trading in New York, as happened during the 1987 crash? The derivative market can no longer operate if the underlying cash market has stopped or if trades on the underlying market cannot be recorded sufficiently quickly. Where is the market being made? In New York or Chicago? And, if the index can be traded in Chicago, ultimately it can be traded in London, Frankfurt, Tokyo or wherever a market is developed, taking the market well beyond the aegis of purely US national regulation. The regulators have to try not only to deal with the competitiveness issues between exchanges and between firms – the need for sound, reliable and transparent markets, and the need to protect the consumer in varying degrees, whether the professional or the retail consumer – but also to ensure that the innovations themselves make sense in the evolving financial and economic environment.

Derivative products do not have to develop outside the market where the cash market is, but, from an end-of-geography point of view, the importance of the derivative market trend is that it allows companies' stocks and markets' indices to be traded in other locations, on other exchanges and on the screen. For the international or global firm, the shift does not matter if access can be obtained to the futures and options markets. The regulators, however, are faced with a more difficult problem. Each regulatory agency or exchange management holds sway over a certain market area, often defined within a geographically defined territory. Regulatory turf is as jealously guarded as market share is protected by the private company or firm. The derivative market requires there to be an increasing degree of cooperation between the different regulators and even a redefinition of authority.

From floor to screen
The development of derivative markets, made possible through computerization and the IT revolution, has a powerful effect on regulatory structures and on the relative positions of stock exchanges. There has, however, been a more visible shift in market behaviour as a result of the IT revolution: the demise of trading floors and the burgeoning growth of computer-based trading floors and telephone trading.

The extent to which this truly changes the fundamental structure of markets, as opposed to being just a highly visible cosmetic change, depends in part on how prices are made. In any market there are basically two ways in which supply and demand for securities are priced: either there are market makers to quote, buy and sell prices at which the market can deal (the market maker ultimately taking the risk of mispricing and having to hold a certain inventory of stock for trading), or no firm prices are quoted but buy and sell orders are matched as they are placed (order-driven systems). The more liquid the market, the more the market makers can be assured that there will be plenty of buy and sell orders. In a thin market, for less well-known stocks, the market maker may be taking a larger risk in making firm quotations. On the traditional stock exchange floors, the market maker could more easily perceive the trading universe and keep in touch with market sentiment. On a computer-based system, the market maker becomes more wary of quoting firm prices in size on the screen. As a result, the transition from floor trading to screen trading is not a simple one, especially for less-liquid securities. For currencies, and interest-rate instruments, where there is much greater depth to the market, screen trading is far more acceptable.

At the same time that this switch to computer-based trading is being contemplated, there is the greater dominance of the institutional trader to consider. More trades tend to be made over the telephone by large players, avoiding the need for the market maker to be making constant prices (i.e. the order-driven market can work over the telephone). The computer becomes the place where the trade is recorded, rather than the place where the trade is transacted. Thus, although in the longer term the potential to switch from physical floor trading to computer-based trading must be one of the most powerful end-of-geography forces, altering the spatial geography of the markets, this shift should not be over-dramatized.

There is a further aspect of the switch to computers that may need to be treated carefully. Markets depend on the flow of good information. We have stressed how the IT revolution has radically altered the speed at which information can be processed and communicated. But there is a certain class of information that cannot be so easily computerized: the information that is communicated in personal conversation, the aside here, the comment there. There is a range of information that players will not put down in black and white, or onto the screen. Often that information will be obtained only by being close to the market, often physically close to those who know. A great deal of the research into companies will be located close to the companies' operations, so that research expertise will still be biased, geographically, to the home base. For company information, this flow of data is probably far more important than information on currencies or money, as local knowledge tends to be more important on companies. Monetary instruments are far closer to the commodity definition than are companies. Hence stock exchanges that aim to retain control over local company trading have a much better chance of succeeding in this plan than in trying to retain an edge over trading, say, the Bund.

In short, the most visible and dramatic manifestations of change in the securities field, such as the closure of the old traditional stock-exchange floors and the development of banks of computer screens, may have a less immediate impact than might be thought. It is the more complex changes wrought by the development of innovative and derivative pro- ducts that are leading to the greatest changes and posing the really acute territorial questions for regulatory authorities.

6
THE GLOBAL
RETAIL CHALLENGE

Does globalization apply to retail finance as much as to wholesale finance? A great deal of the discussion so far has focused on wholesale markets: the global euromarkets, the FX market, the global US Treasury bond market, the securities markets, Big Bangs and the competition between stock exchanges. Global players deal in large amounts and complex instruments. Global investors are either institutions or are extremely rich. Is the end of geography a wholesale market story, of only passing interest to the retail sector?

The answer is no: globalization is an extremely important issue for retail markets, even if the process is less advanced in retail sectors, in many ways, than in wholesale markets. Indeed, as far as regulation is concerned, globalization, integration and the end-of-geography challenge may have a greater effect in retail than in wholesale markets in the coming years, especially in Europe (the end of geography on a regional basis). Let us turn first to the issue of location with respect to retail finance, and then examine the wholesale/retail distinction with respect to globalization's two driving forces: information technology and the regulation of markets.

Location

It is undeniable that for retail markets the need to be local, to be physically close to the market and to the client, will be much more important than in wholesale markets. The reasons are obvious and centre primarily on the needs and preferences of the customer. The retail client will, in the main, confine his or her interests and activities to those that are close to home, and the majority of transactions will take place in the domestic market, even though a high proportion of people, at least in industrial economies, will have a need over time for international payments services of one sort or another, mainly for tourism-related purposes. The wholesale client, on the other hand, will be much more likely to engage in international transactions and trade.

The retail client will also be more likely to want to have a physical connection with the provider of financial services, whether meeting a financial adviser or dealing with the bank. Even visiting the ATM requires making a physical connection. In the future, of course, the connections may extend over the telephone to a greater extent and home banking may become more widespread, with consumers having their own terminals at home (although it may be some time before cash can be delivered at home!). Undeniably, the physical connection is becoming looser for the retail client, but it is not happening so quickly as to build a strong end-of-geography thesis on that trend alone.

The link between ownership and location raises additional questions. Many would argue that for local businesses dealing with a local trusted banker is preferable to dealing with an out-of-town 'big-city' banker, let alone a foreign banker. Certainly the US banking system is built upon the local bank structure. Yet increasingly the local, home-town bank is being owned by 'foreigners', whether out of town, out of state, or out of the country. A classic example is the Australian ownership of the Yorkshire Bank in the United Kingdom. (Perhaps of all the counties in the United Kingdom, Yorkshire is the most insular, and the irony is underlined if we note that Yorkshire's pride in its cricket is perhaps one of its most deeply rooted expressions of that insularity: to be thus owned by a bank from England's historic cricketing rival strikes at all things Yorkshire.)

If the retail consumer places a great deal of store in local connections, how will this tally with the increasing likelihood that, in today's global financial markets, what may appear local may be far from it? For wholesale markets, participants not only will be more used to such global integration; they are likely to be better informed as to the extent of integration. Now many of the good citizens of Yorkshire may be fully aware of the new ownership of the local bank (and US readers should be aware that, in the United Kingdom, local banks are not the majority players even in local areas: the 'national' clearing banks have a large share of the market), but will they be fully aware of the parentage of institutions after 1992, when an increasingly complex web of ownership is likely to develop, not only in banking but in other services, such as insurance. After 1992, any firm will be able to solicit business in York-shire, and, if that firm has any sense at all, it will at least look local even if it is headquartered at the far side of the European continent. Ultimately, what is in a name? Crédit Lyonnais, the Midland Bank, the Bank of Nova Scotia and the Dresdner Bank have one thing in common: none of them is headquartered in its place of origin!*

Thus, obviously location matters a lot in retail finance, and barriers of culture, language and custom will remain, whatever the brave new world of technology and global money. The seller of cross-border retail serv-ices is likely to encounter many more cultural barriers than the seller of wholesale services. Local product delivery is likely to prevail in retail markets, whereas location of the delivery is more flexible for the whole-sale client. Retail product design will need to be locally tailored. But how far the cultural barriers remain is the issue we need to address. The answers may be found in examining the ways in which our twin forces of IT and regulation affect the retail sector.

Information technology and the retail sector
General comments on the ways in which information technology affects the retail sector, from ATMs to the future prospect of home banking, were already made in the opening dicussion on IT. Here let us focus specifically on where the differences lie between the impact of IT on the retail sector and that on the wholesale sector.

The impact comes in two ways: first on the customer/firm relation-ship; and, second, on the organization of the firm itself. The two are interlinked. The central change is that the contact between the firm and the customer is becoming more and more dependent on communications by technology. How far this trend will advance will depend on: (a) how reliable the technology is; (b) how far the customer is willing to use technology in a business in which trust and confidence are important; (c) how far the customer is prepared to invest in technology (clearly a major obstacle to the growth of home banking: hence the Minitel project in France has involved considerable gifts of technology by the services provider); (d) how far technology enables the firm to offer more services to the customer; (e) how technology changes the pricing of retail finan-cial services to the customer; and (f) how far the financial industry is willing to develop, say, the payments networks to offer the customer a wider service, especially wider in terms of geographical coverage.

*I am indebted to Charles Kindelburger for drawing this to my attention.

The introduction of ATMs provides illustrations of most of these aspects: the error rate of ATMs has to be sufficiently low to encourage the customer to use the service. Anecdotal evidence suggests that customer resistance is significant, but will be overcome in time, as habits change. Clearly, ATMs do offer customers wider access to financial services, such as cash withdrawal in more locations on a 24-hour basis. Introduction of ATMs has also involved considerable networking arrangements between banks to offer customers reciprocal services at different banks' outlets. A similar cooperative approach is being developed in the use of other electronic services, such as EFTPOS/debit card systems. At the retail level, of course, the sales outlet also has to be a key partner in the process, investing in the technology to use the financial payments system, whether electronic or through paper-based credit card systems.

But much of this relates to the provision of services within confined geographical areas of domestic, local banking; technology also opens up wider geographical areas for the retail sector. In the EC, there are still considerable restrictions on consumer financial services, in so far as cheques cannot be cashed easily outside the national clearing system, although the consumer does have the option, more and more, of using credit and charge cards for making payments in other countries, as well as travellers cheques. But more straightforward payments to other individuals is more difficult, inconvenient and expensive. This relates of course not so much to the multiplicity of currencies (although that does not help) but to the separation of retail clearing systems. In just the same way, the US consumer faces restrictions because of the absence of nationwide banking in the United States, despite the single currency. Clearly there has never been any real technological barrier to overcome in widening payments systems, except the cost of international communications. The barriers exist much more as a result of the separation of the systems and the lack of incentive to change these systems.

In both the United States and Europe the pressure for change is coming, as a result of a combination of factors: in Europe there is a demand for more cross-border services as integration occurs on other fronts; and in the United States the restructuring of banking, in part to improve profitability, is incorporating wider geographical organizations, mainly at the regional level, but the process continues nationwide. The ending of restrictions on interstate banking is one of the less controversial reform areas, *pace* the strong small bank lobby.

Which brings us to the organizational pressures. What will drive banks and other financial services companies to widen their geographical horizons in retail markets? Here the driving force clearly comes from the economics of banking, allied to the underlying integration of economies. There are tremendous pressures on banks in particular to rebuild the profitability of their business: profits are being squeezed by the loss of free money in the form of non-interest-bearing current or checking accounts, as a result of the competition for private savings from non-banks (securitization of savings); profitability is being squeezed by the higher capital costs of banking; profits are being squeezed by greater competition from foreign institutions in domestic markets (hence access to clearing systems remains a key local defence); and, of course, securitization of assets, hurting the lending business, is very strong. All these pressures have a special influence on the pricing of retail financial services. The competition can attack the business of banks by singling out areas for special attention, on a function-by-function basis, on a product-by-product basis. The profitability of retail banking is particularly vulnerable in this regard, as a result of the higher degree of cross-subsidization that occurs in retail as opposed to wholesale banking.

Thus the deposit base of banks comes under competition from mutual funds and other collective investment instruments (as well as from other types of banks, such as building societies, post offices, savings and loans). The competition can often offer more competitive terms as a result of their own different cost structures. Of course, banks themselves are not powerless to respond by, say, lending to customers which may have been a specialist 'preserve' of other institutions – the competition in the UK mortgage market is a good recent example. But the effect of such product-by-product competition is to reduce the profit margin in each product, and, where that product has had a large margin allowing other products to be subsidized, the effect is felt throughout the bank (the loss of free deposits is clearly the most obvious example). What this means is that retail banking *is* significantly affected by globalization trends, even if a strong sense of locality will be retained as far as the attitude of customers is concerned. The changes in the economics of banking will mean that the customer will be offered different services, at more competitive prices.

There are also many behind-the-scenes changes that are affecting the retail financial services industry, involving global developments, whether the customer realizes it or not. As the banking industry deals with new competitive pressures, it seeks new economies of scale and scope. Such economies are promoted by new technologies on the operational 'back-office' part of the business, as important for retail business services as for wholesale business.

In practice, the technology offers the provider of financial services a widening choice of locations for systems support. An interesting example is provided by the charge card authorization process at American Express. Once upon a time, all card authorizations were processed through Phoenix, Arizona (centralization on a global scale). Today, however, all card usage in Europe would be processed through the centre in Brighton, England, even for, say, a dollar card issued to an Argentinian card-holder. The data bases are interchangeable from one regional centre to another. Thus technology allows a global service to be spread across several regional centres: globalization with less centralization. As far as the customer is concerned, all contact is with the sales clerk at the check-out desk. But as far as the service is concerned, its costing is very much tied to the economies of scale that can now be achieved with good, cheap global communications. No one asked the consumer, although of course the whole process has to pass muster with laws affecting the cross-border interchange of information. This use of technology is not confined to finance: airline ticketing for agencies in the United States are often carried out in the Caribbean, and other examples of global technological interface could be cited. Again, the point is that this is a phenomenon affecting the provision as much of retail services as of wholesale services.

Protecting the consumer
The primary regulatory aspect for the retail sector is the protection of the consumer from the possible adverse aspects of change, even though change also brings benefits to consumers (especially if the consumer has long suffered from so-called pricing cartels). Is the retail sector ready for globalization and integration? Products may still have to be delivered locally, preserving the idea of geography in one sense; but, as those products become global and are provided by 'foreign' banks and suppliers, how will regulators be able to control quality and protect the consumer in the ways deemed necessary? It is quite possible that regulation of retail financial services, in the global and regional framework, will prove to be one of the most difficult areas in coming years.

For example, as the EC integrates, how do the authorities ensure quality across its extent and protect the consumer from unscrupulous 'foreigners', or from less well-regulated firms from other regulatory jurisdictions? At present the difference between domestic and foreign-owned firms may not be a great problem, although the BCCI affair has raised the issue rather earlier than perhaps expected. In ten years' time, it is quite likely that most consumers will neither be aware of the nationality of the financial firm nor be able to say whether the new instrument was a local invention or a foreign import.

These issues are of particular importance in the retail sector, especially if credence is given to the idea that the consumer needs to be given a special degree of protection. What is happening in consumer financial services is very similar to what has occurred over the years in goods markets, where imports of goods and the quality control thereof have long been customary. The safety net is never complete, as every warning about dangerous children's toys from some part of the world bears witness. Such publicity has tended, over time, to force the country of origin to police its own producers, which is, of course, in the interest of all producers from that country. Long gone are the days when Japanese hi-fi and cars were considered shoddy goods. In many respects finance and the toys market are no different from one another: the potential losses to the consumer can be immense in both instances. However, the transparency of financial products is much less than that of other goods: the consumer has a much better chance, on the whole, of distinguishing between safe and unsafe toys, well-made and shoddy goods, and assessing their price/value relationship. Financial products are far harder to assess (hence of course the tendency of financial risks in the consumer area to be socialized through deposit insurance schemes, etc.).

To some extent, this issue is one of degree. Although there are good reasons to pay special attention to the need to protect consumers of financial services, there is also a need to ensure that these consumers recognize some of the responsibilities to look after themselves – *caveat emptor*, to a degree. At the wholesale level, the customer is seen as being able, in many cases, to obtain and use the same amount of information as the provider. At the retail end, in stark contrast, the customer is almost always smaller and less well informed than the provider of the service, and customer power can be expressed only in the aggregate: the regulator often represents the interests of the consumer at the aggregate level.

But integration, innovation, liberalization and globalization mean that in the coming years, in Europe and elsewhere, the consumer is going to be faced with a sharp increase in the number of tempting offers from unfamiliar sellers and, more importantly, a widening range of financial products (especially in insurance/savings products), delivered in new ways, and at a time when many sections of the community will have to manage their own affairs as the state reduces its welfare role. The 1988

Cecchini report on the benefits of the single market underlined the importance of all this to the retail consumer of financial services in its assessment that a full one-third of the economic benefits of the 1992 programme are expected to come from the cost-reduction in retail financial services, as a result of greater transparency and competition, especially where retail cartels are broken up. That may not sound as if the reaction has to be to protect the consumer, but there is no free lunch. If Cecchini is right (another issue entirely), financial firms will have to compete for retail market share far more aggressively, and aggressive competition can be a mixed blessing for the consumer. Are we ready for that consequence of the end of geography? Some already see the interests of the consumer and the supposed benefits diminishing (see Mitchell, 1991).

In the retail sector, a major limiting factor to the integration/globalization process is likely to be the continuing national, cultural, linguistic, social and other geographical characteristics. In the EC, after the first wave of cross-border mergers and acquisitions and alliances, there has been a marked lull. Pacts between large retail players have emerged. It will be considerably harder for foreign firms to break into established retail markets, where perhaps the customer is more conservative, than to break into wholesale markets (and gaining market share in domestic corporate lending is also extremely difficult for outsiders). As noted earlier, the introduction of new technology into the retail arena takes a long time, longer than in wholesale markets. In the United Kingdom, for example, although many people take the ATM for granted as a highly convenient means of obtaining cash, a high proportion of retail customers still refuse to use ATMs. Extension of the ATM to deliver more financial services is in the pipeline, but there is still a long way to go. Progress can also be slowed by the various barriers to connect ATMs, especially across borders. Such connections have to be made at a time when there is growing competition among the financial firms who have a certain interest in retaining control over local markets and slowing, for mutual benefit, the integration process. Technology has to be reliable: nothing frustrates and irritates the customer more than being 'cheated' by a machine and finding redress hard to get. None the less, as convenience and cost considerations gradually help to shift consumer behaviour, it would seem to be inevitable that more integration across borders will take place in retail markets.

Just how the retail user obtains the best service is open to debate, as is illustrated by a final example from share dealing (an area we have perhaps underplayed relative to banking services). There is a concern that the growing institutionalization of stock markets is pricing the retail user out of the market. At the same time, there has been a desire (e.g. in the United Kingdom) to attract more personal savings to the stock markets (although the bulk of the increase has come from the special case of the privatization of publicly owned assets). The economics of share dealing may suggest that individual share dealing is not going to become the pattern of the future, being relatively expensive for trades to be made on an individual basis. This conclusion suggests that collective investments will proliferate, the consumer's savings being invested in products run by the large investment institutions, a trend that would further reinforce the power of the institutions.

7

THE LESSONS FROM EUROPE

The European experience, especially within the European Community, provides a valuable laboratory within which to examine the end-of-geography debate. Many aspects of the move towards greater integration in Europe (economic, monetary, social and political) are special to Europe and are not presented in such intensity elsewhere in the world. Equally, many of the obstacles to the end of geography also exist in Europe: cultural barriers, language barriers, historical barriers. Yet there is a degree of physical integration possible, thanks to geography, which is not so easily applicable elsewhere. It is of course no accident that most trade blocs do have an underlying geographical basis.

The European story is examined here in two parts: the macroeconomic issues and the micro- issues. There is then a concluding section, bringing the two sides together.

The macro story

Why European integration now? The short answer is: Because of the practical progress to date *and* because of the end of geography. Europe has been working towards greater integration since the early 1950s, and Economic and Monetary Union (EMU) has been on the formal agenda since the 1969 presentation to the EC Hague summit of the Werner Report proposals, which aimed at economic and monetary union by 1980. Whatever the setbacks and the amount of progress still to be made, considerable advances have been made towards the EC's stated goals: not only is the EC still converging, but applications for membership have increased sharply; the EMS has confounded the sceptics; the single market programme has accelerated the integration process; political and economic union are on the active agenda. That the timetable for EMU, if it comes into reality, will have slipped twenty years from the original target date need not be seen as a particular mark of failure. The delay offers an object lesson in the gap between theory and practice, the delay between the statement of an ambition and its completion. In fact, the acceleration towards EMU in the late twentieth century derives from the growing importance of our end-of-geography forces. More freely flowing capital, deregulation and improved information technology all reduce barriers wherever they exist. The EC happens to be the arena in which these forces meet the most receptive response.

The European chronology

In the 1950s, the integration process was based upon a strong desire to build a secure postwar economy on the continent, especially among the war-ravaged economies, and particularly involving France and Germany. The United Kingdom was a possible partner, but was sidetracked by its own reorientation away from its 'global' empire role. By the end of the 1960s, the Six (Belgium, France, the Federal Republic of Germany, Italy, Luxembourg and the Netherlands) had shown sufficient strength to suggest that the customs union was of major benefit and that the costs of exclusion for others could be serious. Success encouraged the Six to look to the more ambitious stage of EMU (e.g. the Werner Report). By 1971, the EC's success was encouraging the United Kingdom, Denmark and Ireland to join. During the 1970s the return to democracy in the poorer states of Greece, Portugal and Spain led to their eventual membership and underlined the EC idea of a club of democratic economies (now, in the 1990s, being again reinforced vis-à-vis Eastern Europe).

The 1970s, however, was not a successful decade for EC integration, despite the progress in widening membership. EMU was thrown off track by economic crisis, triggered by the 1973–4 oil shock. But, by the end of the decade, three important lessons had been learnt, both in Europe and elsewhere in the industrialized world: first, the postwar growth miracle could no longer be taken for granted, implying that the EC had to press forward if it was to gain more from its union; second, the individual weaknesses in European economies were revealed (Eurosclerosis), leading to policy reforms in the early 1980s (especially in the United Kingdom, but also in France after the mistakes of the early Mitterrand years); and, third, the costs of floating exchange rates for business and policymakers were becoming apparent, as the brave new world of floating turned out to be far more volatile and hazardous than had been expected. Something had to be done.

And something was done. The continental countries, led by France and Germany, set up the EMS. The United Kingdom, while eschewing full EMS membership for the next eleven years, abolished exchange controls. The UK route towards integration was in effect an alternative, parallel and even more liberal track towards globalization, opening capital flows not just to and from Europe but also vis-à-vis the rest of the world. By the mid-1980s there was sufficient momentum in place for the continental members to push for the single market programme, to be the next logical step after the customs union. The United Kingdom was able to endorse this new initiative and sign the Single European Act (SEA, 1985) as a further step towards deregulation in Europe. The next stage in the integration process, EMU, aims to take Europe beyond the single market programme and on to the most ambitious path of economic and monetary integration seen in Europe's history, and indeed between any group of nation-states under peacetime conditions.

The case for EMU
The starting economic theory for EMU is that developed in the 1960s as the theory of the optimum currency area, which argues that an optimum currency area requires freedom of movement of capital and labour so that economies can adjust to economic shocks. If this condition applies, then monetary union brings the added advantage of eliminating the transactions costs of exchanging currencies. The EC has moved towards almost complete freedom of movement of capital, which results in part from the long-term end-of-geography conditions. However, movement of labour is likely to remain restricted in practice, not least as a result of language barriers. Thus the optimal currency area arguments fail to provide a particularly convincing case, so further arguments in favour of EMU are needed (set out in the European Commission's 'One market, one money' paper).

The most powerful arguments put forward for EMU come straight from the end-of-geography scenario. It is argued that price stability is becoming increasingly important in running stable economies; that governments must increasingly discipline their financial affairs; that instability in economic relations with other countries, resulting from go-it-alone policies, is even more hazardous than in the past; and all this is due to the mobility of capital and the way in which international capital flows will punish any economy that attempts to get seriously out of line.

Supplementary arguments are given to boost the case: for example, one-product economies might wish to preserve the right to pursue an independent line, since they are then in a position to counteract the occasional shocks (e.g. Texas could have used the devaluation option after the fall in oil prices to prevent a slump in the local economy, but even that is a questionable option); Europe, however, has no such one-product economies. And, it can be argued, the smaller economies of Europe certainly will benefit from more integration, given their already high dependence on economic relations with partner states. Naturally it is the large economies who still entertain desires to retain strong national independence.

But the most important argument for EMU brings us from the macro to the micro economy: that in addition to the static gains from EMU there will be dynamic gains (the basis for this being the work by Baldwin, 1991). The business sector has argued that growth and investment in Europe is hampered by the extent of exchange-rate uncertainty, imposing a cost on business that does not exist in larger integrated economies, such as that of the United States. This fits with all the other single market (i.e. bigger home market) arguments. It was the power of this argument that pushed the EC towards the SEA and the 1992 process. The debate now is whether the single market process itself can be completed without the follow-up from EMU. In practice it will have to move ahead, given that 1992-3 will long predate a single currency, even according to the most ambitious timetables. Of course, US experience reminds us that a single currency does not ensure a single market, but a single currency is seen as necessary to complete a single market. The final pro-EMU argument moves on to the global arena: that EMU will contribute to global stability by establishing a powerful stable third leg for global economic policy and cooperation, with Europe operating alongside the United States and Japan.

Europe has proceeded on a step-by-step process towards these conditions for integration. The time has become riper because of end-of-geography forces: capital mobility is the new factor, facilitated both by the IT revolution and by regulatory change. The final removal of capital controls in 1990 puts more pressure on the EMS to work through policy coordination, without being able to rely on those capital controls that remained (and indeed it can be argued that such controls were becoming largely ineffectual, certainly for wholesale markets, and merely restricting consumer choice by affecting private individuals' flows). The response in Europe of the policymakers has been to accept the end-of-geography challenge rather than resist integration. Both the continental countries and the United Kingdom have reached the same conclusion, though the approaches may differ.

Of course, freer capital mobility is not unique to Europe. Stability in economic growth and the debate over exchange rates are not just European concepts. The difference between Europe and the rest of the world, which determines why Europe can progress apace, lies in the chronology: Europe has more of the necessary ingredients in place to pursue integration (many of which of course relate to geography). But many of the broad principles are the same. Countries abandon some of their 'geography' (otherwise referred to as sovereignty) by getting rid of exchange controls.

The micro story
The European experience also provides an excellent test-case for the micro aspects of integration and globalization, via the creation of the single market. European integration, like global integration, depends critically on the marketplace and competitive forces putting plans into action. Neither EMU nor the single market can be created by administrative fiat. Europe is meeting its end-of-geography challenge by adopting a number of guiding principles, as usual submerged in jargon: 'mutual recognition', 'subsidiarity', 'home-versus-host regulation', 'competition among rules'. (For further discussion on some of these issues, please refer to Wallace and Wilke, 1990, and Woolcock, et al., 1991.) Often the approach accepts that geography will continue to exist and be relevant (e.g. home-versus-host distinctions). In this discussion we shall concentrate on financial market integration.

The principles
In the European context, subsidiarity means that whatever can be decided at the local/national (i.e. subsidiary) level should continue to be decided there, leaving pan- or supraregional/European arrangements/laws to apply only where such overall legislation is necessary. In the financial markets this approach leads on to the concepts of mutual recognition and the home-versus-host approach.

Under the principle of mutual recognition, any financial firm that is licensed for certain financial activities in one EC country will be permitted to perform such functions in any EC country in which that activity is allowed, since its licence will be recognized in all countries. This is very different from the national treatment formula, whereby foreign entities are permitted to perform all activities that national (local) firms are permitted to perform. Mutual recognition is also referred to as the 'single passport' approach: the 'passport' issued by one country is recognized elsewhere and provides free entry throughout the EC. The principle of mutual recognition removes any question of reciprocity being necessary.

Mutual recognition requires mutual respect. Will all countries provide sufficiently high-quality regulation of home institutions to ensure that host countries can be fully satisfied that an EC passport is a sign of quality (and no threat to consumers or the system)? Related to this is the concern about competition in regulatory laxity, where there may be the risk that some firms may seek to be based in the country with the least stringent rules, and that some regulatory authorities may encourage firms to be based in their jurisdiction by applying an easier set of rules. This latter concern may be effectively dealt with by ensuring that a firm's primary licence is given by the country in which it has the majority of its business, so that if the firm runs into problems there is a good chance that a large part of the problem will land on the mat of the licensing authority (thus making any authority more cautious about issuing licences). As to the evenness of quality of regulation and supervision, there is no easy answer to this question, except that all twelve nations exert peer pressure on each other and on their various regulatory bodies to provide quality and to be alert for attempts to compete for business through regulatory laxity.

The home-versus-host principle divides regulatory and supervisory responsibilities between the home country (where the firm is headquartered) and the host country/ies (where the firm carries out its business). The principle is of particular interest in the end-of-geography context, since it depends upon the geographical separation of responsibilities. The home country is responsible for such things as the licence, appropriate ownership structures and capital adequacy. The host country has authority over the behaviour of the firm in the host marketplace: for example, conduct of business. This approach aims to allow for local cultures and business practices to be respected while at the same time requiring each country to develop licensing supervision that attains some minimum quality level across the Community. In financial terms, the home authority is responsible for solvency issues, the host authority for liquidity.

Over time it will become more difficult to determine just who is the home and who is the host authority. At present most banks and firms have an obvious nationality and natural base: BCCI was a classic exception. What if a bank from a small country builds a larger business in a larger country? For example, it would not be too difficult for a Portuguese bank to build a large portfolio in, say, Spain or France of greater size that its Portuguese business. In the single market this will be likely to happen more and more: the whole point of the single market is to allow and to encourage such expansion of the domestic base of companies, so that 'domestic' means the region and not just the nation. This is not simply a matter of statelessness, but one of having multinational and Europe-wide businesses. In theory even this might not be too difficult to handle (market shares are not going to be jumping around rapidly, and cooperation among supervisors should be sufficient to handle most cases). But at some point it will not be easy to make national distinctions as firms increase their cross-border selling of products and truly ignore national barriers and structures.

The home-versus-host distinction will also become more difficult to make in terms of clearly defining the different responsibilities of each authority. In theory the difference is clear: the home country has responsibility for most things until we come to the conduct of business and respect for local customs. In practice this is supposed to work on the basis of 'when in Rome, do as the Romans do'. However, the whole recent history of finance (and in fact of all integration) shows that local customs and practices are radically altered by the activities of the newcomers. Their own cultures are imported and inevitably lead to debates within each market as to when it is appropriate for imported habits to be permitted. All countries that have experienced large-scale immigration will be fully aware of the impossible dilemmas that arise when the members of a growing minority begin to assert their right to conduct themselves according to their own customs: the arguments are rarely solved in principle; they are solved in the law courts and on the streets. The customs of many nations are now determined by those of former immigrant populations.

The BCCI collapse provides a good example of the home/host dilemmas, posing not just the question of whether the differences in deposit insurance levels should be harmonized (or equalized) in Europe, but also whether the insurance should be provided by the home or the host authority/marketplace. Given that capital adequacy and safety and soundness of firms is supposed to be the responsibility of the home authority, there is a case for deposit insurance, a factor linked to soundness, to be a home-country responsibility. Yet deposit insurance is also part and parcel of the way in which funds are raised in local markets.

Should firms with a more generous deposit insurance scheme be allowed to compete in other markets in which the system may be different? The bottom line on this looks likely to be a more rapid move towards harmonization of the deposit insurance levels throughout Europe, to reduce the inequalities and to finess of the home/host problem.

A broader set of problems arises when different types of financial market structures begin to merge in the single market. There are straightforward differences of opinion as to which rule or system is best, or most efficient, and what type of financial market structure is optimal. For example, the German form of universal banking, involving close company/bank ties as well as having integrated financial services (*allfinanz*) firms, is not practised in the same way in the United Kingdom: a priori, neither can be said to be better or worse, especially as both systems are ingrained in the whole corporate and banking structure of each economy. Yet both systems will have to work alongside each other and increasingly be integrated with each other as the single market becomes a reality. Europe will certainly be a valuable test-case for this aspect of integration and globalization, as other financial systems in the United States and Japan pursue reform and make the comparison with different systems.

It is to cope with this genuine difference of approach, which cannot be effectively decided through the process of directive and negotiation, that 'competition among rules' is pursued: i.e., let the markets and their accompanying rule-makers compete in open and fair competition, and see how firms and regulators and consumers act. It is this competitive approach to integration that most suits the United Kingdom, which is to a degree confident that relative openness has not in the past handicapped its institutions. At the same time, the relatively closed cartel system that exists in Germany and elsewhere is more obviously in conflict with the principles of openness and transparency. Yet, as discussed earlier, the obvious relative success of the German economy to date suggests that the German system will not be abandoned lightly and certainly not just through negotiation.

Other end-of-geography issues arise in the micro/market aspects of European integration, some of which have already been explored elsewhere in this study: the competition between national stock markets, which has been referred to as the internationalist versus the '*vive la géographie*' approach, is a classic example of how different national and market interests are seeking to ensure that their market survives in the new Europe, and they are having to make the judgment as to which type of system will work in practice. There has already been a flurry of cross-border mergers and acquisitions as financial firms react to the end-of-geography challenge. The prospect of easier access to other markets, without the extra layer of bureaucracy and organizational structure that separate markets require, is a welcome opportunity, but one that also raises the competitive stakes, since other firms can enter home markets more easily. The reactions of the private sector already reveal a readiness to adapt, but even so it is likely that the full flood of such integration and cross-border ownership has yet to occur. Cross-ownership stakes are being negotiated for strategic reasons by some of the larger European banks, which are in part recognizing the reality that none of the larger players are ready to make a head-on pitch for other national domestic retail markets, but that eventually they will. In the meantime it is in the mutual interests of the banks to seek passive alliances.

As mergers and acquisitions develop, governments will have to decide whether they need to support national champions in banking and finance. Four years ago the Governor of the Bank of England stated that it ran 'counter to commonsense' that the core of the British financial system should pass into foreign hands (Leigh-Pemberton, 1987). Slowly this approach, if not the sentiment, is likely to change. Not only is such an approach contrary to EC rules and understandings; the very definition of the 'core banking' structure is steadily changing. Parts of the core might welcome an addition of capital from outside, while new core banks have emerged (as building societies become banks). But, to be realistic, almost every European country is likely to be reluctant to see its core financial sector being dominated by foreign (even if other European) firms.

For European consumers, the end of geography is seen as both a boon and a threat. On the benefit side, the cost of financial services is forecast to drop sharply, as noted earlier, accounting for one-third of the benefits of the single market. In practice these cost savings may not occur quite so quickly: it is assumed that a number of the costs, such as foreign exchange translation for tourists, will just disappear. However, a strong feature of retail financial costs everywhere is in the extent of cross-subsidization of services, notably the ability of many banks to perform services for nothing, being remunerated by interest-free chequeing accounts. Financial market innovation and competition by non-banks and technology are rapidly eroding these free balances and forcing banks to unbundle services, to apply charges more directly to specific services and to reduce the amount of cross-subsidization. The foreign currency translation services, for example, often simultaneously provide for a payments service: cashing travellers cheques in the single currency market of the United States still attracts a cost.

A single currency or even fixed exchange rates in Europe will not in themselves alter the fragmented state of European retail banking: only with pan-European payments systems and firms will the consumer be able to transfer money as easily from one account in Europe to another, as is currently possible within nation-states. This integration can now be effected more rapidly that in the past, thanks to the new technologies, which, being able to ignore geographical boundaries, means that there is no practical reason why any transference of money should not be made anywhere in the EC. But it will require the establishment of a more integrated payments system.

For consumers, the integration process in Europe will also mean a wider range of services being offered as firms in each country look for opportunities in other economies. There is, for example, a marked difference in the amount of insurance premia paid in each country, suggesting untapped possibilities in some markets and perhaps saturation elsewhere. However, the selling of insurance-related products is often an integral part of an economy's basic mix of personal savings products: in the case of Italy, for example, the apparent lack of purchase of insurance products is more to do with the abundance of tax-efficient savings opportunities offered by the Treasury than as a result of a radically different attitude of South Europeans to insurance.

Conclusion: lessons from Europe
The relevance of the EC process emerges in several ways:

(1) The end of geography is all about the reduction of barriers: the EC process is all about the reduction of internal barriers within the single market, and hopefully not just replacing them with barriers around the EC itself.

(2) The end of geography is a particularly important issue in the realm of finance: the EC process depends crucially on progress in the financial sector, not just because of the pivotal importance of monetary integration. The EC debate already involves the issue of the restructuring of the equity markets, especially in terms of location and geographical scope; it involves the debate over the location of financial centres; and it provides the first major test of the workability of coordinated regulations that still distinguish between location (i.e. the home-versus-host distinction).

(3) The EC also pits differing types of financial structure against one another, not just universal banking versus more separated structures, but also systems with high degrees of national ownership, differing bank/ commerce links and those with a different balance of power between banking and securities firms.

(4) The EC process involves integration of both retail and wholesale sectors, and thus is in advance of the more global developments, which still tend to emphasize integration of wholesale markets. Of course, what may be possible in the regional environment may be less feasible globally, since the geographical aspect is more restricted to the region.

(5) The EC process is one of both micro and macro integration, dependent on the integration of governments' economic policies as well as on the development of Europe-wide economies of scale for the firm.

There are also a number of important differences between the EC process and the global process:

(1) Integration in Europe goes further than the pace of integration at the global level: the EC is establishing a legal framework beyond that of the nation-state, developing agreements, procedures and accords on a regional and supranational basis (albeit still with a strong, vital element of national laws via the so-called principle of subsidiarity). In contrast, no such global regulatory structure is being contemplated, although there is an increasing effort to coordinate and harmonize laws across borders, especially for international business (as per the BIS rules on capital adequacy).

(2) There is strong political and broad economic impetus behind the European process, which hardly exists globally. EC financial integration is built upon the whole EC 1992 process and the drive for greater political and economic integration, providing a strong momentum and pressure for integration that does not exist across the globe. In contrast, there is no formal Global 2000 integration process at work to match EC 1992 or the EMU effort.

(3) The European process has a chance of going much deeper than integration of finance across the globe, especially in terms of the integration of retail financial markets. Indeed, for retail finance (in contrast to wholesale markets), the limits to the end of geography are quite restricted (except for the higher-income private financial services) and are less likely to extend beyond regions, except for travel-related financial services.

(4) Geography is undeniably important to the EC process, making possible the economic and political integration process and stemming from historical rivalry (and now from the aim of peaceful coexistence). The attitude of each EC nation is influenced by geography, from the persistence of the British in seeing themselves as somewhat separate (as an island, almost on the periphery) to the Janus-like attitude of the Germans to their neighbours to the east and west. Yet geographical proximity does not, of course, ensure integration. Borders arise where differences arise, even if the exact drawing of the border will often run through 'grey' areas. There are very real reasons why Europe is divided into separate nations, and no amount of wishful thinking, information technology or deregulation is going to eliminate history so quickly.

(5) Finally, the EC process has a further dimension because it is a regional, not a global process: the Community, as a collectivity, has external relations with other regions, and there is at least the possibility of developing some kind of European identity. There is no such collective external relations aspect to global integration. In practice, Europe's identity and external boundaries will remain difficult to define as the Community widens. Widening could slow the deepening process, but the option of keeping to the twelve has probably passed into history. Indeed, to a great extent, the process of regionalization is merely a sub-process of globalization, so there is little prospect of stopping the integration process at the boundaries of the region. To some degree, of course, the world may be moving more towards financial regionalism (see Kaufman, 1991) than towards globalism. A number of European aims already look ambitious for Europe and may look even more utopian on a global scale.

8

EVERYBODY HAS TO BE SOMEWHERE: THE NEW DETERMINANTS OF LOCATION

In theory, the end of geography should mean that location no longer matters. Yet, 'Everybody has to be somewhere,' as Spike Milligan once put it so eloquently in response to the standard question: 'What are you doing here?'. Location still exists, even though electronic markets make that location more difficult to identify in traditional geographical ways. Firms, individuals, markets, even products, have to have a sense of place. This chapter examines the question of location from two perspectives: that of financial centres, and that of the financial firm.

Financial centres
The most lively debate as to location focuses on the role and location of financial centres, especially those with international pretensions. Studies abound on the rival attractions of London, Frankfurt, Paris, Hong Kong and Singapore, New York and Chicago, Beirut and Bahrain, Tokyo and Osaka, with very strong public and private interest groups supporting such studies. Financial centres mean jobs for the city in question (finance is like the Olympic Games in this regard: it tends to be the city not the nation that competes for the activity). There is also expected to be some benefit for the economy and companies of the country in which the financial centre is located, although London has long been criticized for paying insufficient attention to UK interests, and its contribution to the invisibles line on the balance of payments tends to be the main apparent benefit to the nation. Centres compete not only internationally but also with other cities and regional centres in each economy.

Quite clearly, financial centres develop in order to bring together in one convenient location the wide range of talents and knowledge needed to develop financial markets. Strength in breadth and depth has always been important. London, to take the pre-eminent international example, drew strength from the fact that so many markets were located in a small area: commodity markets, precious metals markets, the stock market, currency markets (especially when based on sterling as a reserve currency) and the world's biggest insurance market. No other centre could boast such a collection. Since markets thrive on the rapid interchange of information, so a marketplace such as London developed, and the location of the world's leading news services in London has been an additional key factor. The same principles apply to all markets, from the smallest street-market to the London Stock Exchange (itself founded where people met, for coffee). As the markets developed, so they attracted the necessary ancillary services, notably legal services, accounting and auditing skills, and, in today's world, public relations and advertising expertise. Geography has traditionally had a lot to do with the location of financial centres and, indeed, as the label the Square Mile bore witness, has even defined the limits of the financial centre. Elsewhere we have seen expertise confined to very specific locations, as in the Jewish areas of European cities in the past, or in the entrepôt islands of Hong Kong and Singapore, or in the islands of the Caribbean (where the true location of the service was perhaps more questionable: a brass plate is the legal, not the actual, location).

What happens under end-of-geography conditions? There are two counterforces: on one side it can be argued that financial centres are no longer needed, since communications allow experts to work together on the telephone, over the fax and through computer-linked trading. For every example of integration there exists a counterbalancing example of growing specialization and fragmentation in markets. Even London is no longer confined to the Square Mile. The other side of the argument suggests that there should be more concentration of expertise in centres: thanks to communications, there are even greater possibilities to develop economies of scale through concentrating markets in one location, selling the same product from one centre across an even greater area. Perhaps we need only three major centres, one to cover each of the three main time zones (despite the attempts to make even time zones irrelevant through 24-hour trading).

The divergent forces are both consistent with the end of geography and with each other, reflecting an important tension in the dynamics of change. Confusion arises only if we confuse production with marketing and delivery, back-office with front-office services and if we forget the laws of comparative advantage. As free trade literature and experience demonstrates, free trade leads to specialization and product differentiation, as competing firms hone their competitive edge. Removal of barriers increases the tradability of financial products and increases the volume of trade. (For a discussion of the trade and tradability aspects, see Hoekman and Sauvé, 1991). Level playing-fields make the competition keener, not duller. The more nearly equal each producer's competitive position becomes, the more sensitive are the markets to small differences in production costs and consumer tastes, and the more important it is that comparative advantages are recognized and exploited.

In practice this means that pools of specialist expertise will continue in some financial centres, with technology making it easier to link those pools with others outside the financial centre, often closer to the market. At times this outreach will be important because of the remaining geography, involving different tastes and languages, etc., in different market-places. As British companies have already shown, selling insurance to the Italian market is easier said than done, even if the laws are making it more and more possible. At the same time, certain markets will not be able to stop other centres competing for their own business, as we see in stock markets, in the competition for different bond, futures and option contracts. Centres will compete, and in fact are likely to proliferate in terms of the delivery and selling functions, as players compete to get as close as possible to the client, even if the products are developed elsewhere. The increased volume of trading means that financial centres are not competing for a fixed amount of business: the volume of business is likely to increase as more players (investors included) have access to more markets and as companies can be brought to market in more countries.

A market is, of course, one of the primary expressions of geography, being the meeting-place for buyers and sellers, for producers and consumers, and being the location of the middlemen, the traders. Furthermore, and very relevant for the end-of-geography challenge, regulations are focused on markets. The idea that conduct-of-business patterns alter from market to market implies different conduct according to geography. Markets develop a close affinity with other aspects of their location, from nationality issues (or regional issues) to other local characteristics and customs. Firms have to operate in markets. The Big Bangs were all about the opening-up of specific markets, located in previously restricted areas, to outsiders.

Certain activities will still be transacted within a relatively limited physical area, in which a collection of expertise is valuable: corporate finance, for example, requires close negotiation involving a number of experts, such as bankers and lawyers. The communications between the principals can be conducted a great deal over the telephone, but they are not trading a simple product, and the sharing of information is not always easily done outside the personal contact, however sophisticated the technology. Where deals require the personal touch, and where charisma is important (for deal-making and, of course, marketing), location of the players will still matter. It is often eyeball-to-eyeball stuff, all night if need be. Such 24-hour business is not an alien concept to those who have put loan documentation together over the years. However, even these deals bring with them additional services that can be provided through non-personal means.

Retail markets will retain a strong local aspect, for obvious reasons, although in this area more ATM-based communication can be expected to develop between the customer and the service provider. Mail-order selling of financial products may well increase, especially in Europe as the regional retail market opens up, and perhaps in the United States as nationwide banking emerges. In Japan, also, the securities houses fear that it is the extensive branch networks of the larger banks that threaten their business if banks obtain a strong foothold in the retail securities business. There are, of course, some global retail products, such as travellers cheques and credit cards, which are of added value to the customer because the regular payments system, which is provided through normal cheque payments, does not always work outside the nation (or the even narrower state/region in the United States). These payments products would be under threat in a truly global payments system.

Many wholesale markets of course have already gone global, especially where the product is global. Derivative markets are a direct challenge to existing ideas of geography and to the idea of independent stock markets. The European scene seems set for a more integrated European stock market, despite efforts to maintain local powers. But the process is not just regional, although Globex is at present being used as a communications tool for separate futures and options markets to trade together, eventually there will be greater integration, and markets on both sides of the Atlantic will be brought together.

The future of the stock and other trading markets will ultimately be decided by the attitudes of the member firms of the exchanges, and by the location preferences of these firms. Stock exchanges are generally owned by their member firms, and their principal aim is to make a profit as an exchange and to enable members to make trading profits. Profit in trading is heavily dependent on trading volumes, so growth maximization is a key factor in profit maximization and also creates the necessary depth to markets themselves. In practice, every stock exchange has developed a business niche (large or small), but, like all marketplaces, it is always possible for the trading to move elsewhere. The same analogy would apply for a financial centre. Exchanges try to preserve geography, to ensure that their business does not move elsewhere. But the member firms can move. Thus, if all trading moved from New York to Chicago, that would be bad news for New York itself, but the firms would gradually build up their presence in Chicago.

Yet in an end-of-geography world, in which location is not supposed to matter, why would a market move at all? Markets and traders can, after all, be linked up wherever the necessary technology is installed. The answer, it seems, is that there is still a strong incentive for stock exchanges to be close to the location of the operations of the companies whose shares are traded on the exchange, since research has remained localized (unlike currency research, as discussed earlier). The less global the company, the less 'commodity-like' the product, and the more geography is likely to be retained.

Given that corporate equities have local characteristics, the easiest way for them to develop as global products is as part of the indexed products on the market (i.e., investors believe that they can make a judgment about the Australian economy and buy or sell the Australian stock markets accordingly, but would not make individual stock-picking choices quite so readily). Sometimes there are formal restrictions that require foreign investors to buy the market, not the stock (the rationale for a number of emerging country funds). In addition there will be a local nucleus of investors interested in the local companies. In the longer run, part of the key to the true globalization of stock markets will lie in the globalization of the companies themselves that trade on the exchanges, which will be a slow process.

The decision over the appropriate location also depends upon the development of global systems. A heavy investment in technology is needed before systems reach global proportions. Progress has to be made in several areas: clearing and settlements systems, trading systems, global custody systems, clearing for retail transactions, in-house computerization, and reducing the flow of paper, from cheques to stock certificates.

The London Stock Exchange's TAURUS system, which will put all stock records onto computer and eliminate stock certificates, the so-called 'de-materialization', has taken far longer to put on line than anticipated. In retail markets, ATM networks have to be expanded through new investment. It is in the area of systems that barriers can be put up to prevent the end of geography and to preserve a degree of proprietorial control. Globex-traded products will all be cleared in the 'home' exchange, giving the exchange control over the product even though over time it will be the trading activity, not the clearing, that will count. And there is no reason why networks cannot be developed to provide effective cartels.

Towards the global firm

Financial firms have been among the most enthusiastic supporters of globalism, investing in the new technology to improve their global operations. Those observers that foresee the demise of globalism cite the over-capacity in the major markets and the pulling-back of many firms from the attempt to have a global presence. The truth is, such firms have begun to understand more closely the costs of global presence and the demand for such services. As the barriers between sectors in the financial services industry are taken away, so firms can restructure themselves according to existing and potential markets. There is a great deal of room for different strategies somewhere between that of the super-global universal banking financial firm and the niche/specialist/boutique approach.

Both growth and profit maximization remain the driving forces of firms' behaviour. Only experience can tell us what is the best route to the optimal mix. The optimal strategy also changes according to market conditions and perceived strategic priorities. At times the objectives translate into survival and protection against takeover, at other times into more aggressive expansionism, with profits being in the future, reinforced at the time by rising price/earnings ratios as shareholders second-guess management.

Alongside these geographical issues, financial firms face ongoing business-restructuring questions. Which will be the most profitable financial services business, in terms of the rate of return on capital (the question that shareholders ask)? Where will these businesses be profitable? The same questions then have to be asked in line with growth ambitions. Finally, the firm has to decide on the best way to operate in those markets/businesses, as a global player or as a niche player. Allied to all location issues will be tax considerations, affecting in many cases the location of incorporation rather than of business activities (where such divergences are permitted).

It seems very likely that there will be only a few players in each broad segment of financial services who will be able to call themselves (in all honesty) global businesses. And global business means being able to deliver services across the globe, not necessarily in every corner of the globe, but certainly in the major financial capitals. Delivery means delivery in a timely and competitive way. Gaps in global coverage can still be filled either by network arrangements with other suppliers, or by accepting that the service may not be comprehensive, accepting that some clients will go elsewhere for part of the service. Ultimately, the cost of being non-global will be influenced by the extent to which clients themselves need global delivery, or whether clients themselves, in reality, have less than global needs.

A degree of specialization is likely to persist, with global banks, securities houses, insurance companies and other financial services companies. For each group, the 'global' structure is likely to be tailored to that appropriate for the sector. The global/multinational bank tries to be in as many places as possible. To some extent this is more of a multinational approach than a global, integrated one. The bank offers its customers its services everywhere, and trades on its name and brand worldwide. Its services are likely to be more global in nature in the wholesale business than in the retail sector.

Global securities firms aim at a presence in each of the major securities markets – London, New York and Tokyo – offering 24-hour support and the ability to trade in all the important markets and to raise funds for clients everywhere. Again, at present this is more of a multimarket than an integrated global market approach. However, in so far as clients are trading global portfolios (i.e. the clients themselves are global) then the activity in each market will be linked. However, despite the efforts to develop 24-hour trading in New York and elsewhere, the sheer physical obstacles suggest that, in an end-of-geography world, with the right technology in place, the idea of having to provide a 24-hour service from one physical location is outdated.

The increasingly international and global role of the insurance business is moving into prominence in the financial industry, both in retail markets (in the sale of savings products) and in wholesale markets (driving investment strategies on to the global plane, alongside the world's big pension funds). In the present climate of deregulation and giving the customer greater control over his/her own financial assets and affairs, the consumer is demanding more financial (often savings) products. Insurance, pension and unit-trust-related products account for a high percentage of the financial assets of the consumers. Insurance firms deal in the savings of the consumer, while banks handle transactions, which are the payments services of the consumer. Insurance (and pension) companies are already among the biggest financial services companies and are the biggest institutional investors. Their end of geography is related to the increasing ability to invest in all markets, in the absence of exchange controls and other restrictions, in whatever market offers the best price and liquidity.

Finally, the global reach of companies selling global payments services, such as American Express, depends on being able to service clients everywhere. The product needs to penetrate as many markets as possible, so that it can be used worldwide, and, as already noted, services such as delivery of travellers cheques and use of credit and charge cards has to be global. This does require a presence in markets in the form of a licence to do business. It also requires a global payments systems network, operating through local payments systems.

In addition, there is the possibility of the global conglomerate, of a global firm that combines one or more of the above sectors. For the moment, the global conglomerate has to work within the structure, country by country, sector by sector, specializing in some markets, playing several roles in others. It will be tough to be a truly global conglomerate. At present, of course, many firms are already tempering ambitious global growth plans, whether on the part of banks reducing their international networks, or securities firms withdrawing from markets and locations. The withdrawal of players does not necessarily reduce globalization; rather, it indicates that only a few firms will be able to play the global game and be a force in all major locations.

Alongside these global firms will be the powerful local players, who in the local market may be as strong as the global players, and will be price-setters. Some of these will have tried the global route and withdrawn to reinforce their domestic base. Given that there will still be markets and needs that we can call domestic, this strategy should be workable. Then there will be the smaller players, some offering a degree of global service through a network, without being price-setters in any major market, others being small players in local markets. There are many possible permutations. In fact each firm will be looking for its own special permutation of the general formula.

Undoubtedly the greatest progress towards building the global firm will be in the wholesale and corporate markets. It is unlikely that many, if any, firms can realistically entertain ambitions to be major competitors in all retail markets, although this is more feasible on a regional basis, for which there are likely to be regional economies of scale and scope. It will still be very tough for the 'foreign' player to obtain high-quality access to local retail markets or even to local corporate customers: credit assessment and wooing the best customers cannot be done overnight. The majority of the world's financial firms still have a strong domestic base with a widely varying degree of international operations or of operations outside the home base (which can often be branch or subsidiary business in other local markets). The principal advantage that a foreign firm has over local firms is that the parent of the branch or subsidiary is foreign, and can therefore bring a new dimension into negotiations with the client.

Where a firm attempts to have a large retail presence abroad, that presence is, on the whole, aimed at emulating and outperforming the local financial firms. Competitiveness depends on efficiency (e.g., use of technology that might not be fully available to local competitors, notably in poorer countries) or often on regulations (which may handicap the foreign entrant). One of the key measures of globalization, integration and the end of geography comes where inroads into local retail markets are made by foreign firms, which then lend to local businesses and, less frequently, trade on local markets. The 1980s have seen advances in this direction as foreign firms (especially banks) have operated more widely in the United States, and in Europe some of the largest battles will take place in the retail banking field. Frequently, where these advances take place through acquisition (e.g. the Australian takeover of the Yorkshire Bank), the retail customer is less aware of the change, which at the beginning is primarily one of ownership rather than having any other impact.

If there is a slight shift away from the global approach that was so fashionable in the 1980s it may be because of a re-emphasis on the firm's status within regional markets, where regions represent expanding 'single', integrated markets. Positioning in Europe, in the US market or in Japan is quite likely to be the clearest point of focus for management. Many of the important strategic decisions may still apply to local business. In the United States, the long-awaited reform of the whole financial system offers tremendous rewards for those who get the business mix right, buy/sell the right businesses at the right time and price, and use greater opportunities to develop nationwide banking profitably. In Japan, the key rivalry will be between the securities firms and the banks and between different parts of the segmented banking system: the foreign challenge will be of less importance. The European protagonists will certainly have other European firms in focus. Meanwhile, the forces of globalization, integration and securitization will tend to open the closed systems, assisted by the influence of foreign competition gaining access to domestic markets.

9
ECONOMIC AND POLITICAL INTEGRATION

The primary focus of this paper is financial markets. Yet the end of geography is a theme that can be developed in many arenas, especially with respect to economic and political integration. Although this chapter cannot hope to add significantly to the extensive literature on economic and political integration issues, it is important to draw out the links between the end of geography in finance and other integration and globalization trends. The following analysis will thus fall into three categories: an assessment of where the world economy is going with respect to the broad aspect of economic integration; a discussion of the aspects of integration that link finance and economics more widely; and, finally, a comment on the other major integration items on the global agenda.

Progress towards global integration

A recent appraisal of the progress of economic integration worldwide reached the following broad conclusions (based on ten propositions put forward by David Henderson, 1991): first, integration in the broader economic arena is happening, it will probably continue and it could have large global effects, but we should not get too excited about the pace of integration; second, integration in finance *is* progressing at a faster pace than in other areas; and, third, central to the pace of change is whether governments and people find such changes 'acceptable' – which in the context of this study translates as, are the public and private sectors of our economies ready for the end of geography? Attitudes to labour migration will be a key test of the willingness to allow fuller integration, while creeping protectionism suggests some backsliding in global integration.

The integration of the EC nations, and other European economies eventually, is the best and most far-reaching example of economic integration and is, as discussed, a test-case for a global end of geography. The other major example of integration among developed economies is that between the United States and Canada, to which could be added the growing integration between Australia and New Zealand. In each of these cases, the integration process involves an increasing integration of financial services and currency coordination and is inseparable from trade liberalization between the countries. It is also clear that as each region develops its own new structure, in the economy as a whole as well as in finance, there is a great deal of pressure to ensure that the firms of those regions are competitive worldwide. Competition policy is likely to be one of the most important issues in the end-of-geography challenge.

The link between financial market integration and economic integration undoubtedly will be affected by the attitude taken to a single currency, whether in the EC, the United States and Canada, or Australasia. Market transparency, pricing transparency, and information exchange and usage will be greatly advanced within any single currency area, even though the creation of a single currency area itself does not create a single financial market (as has already been pointed out for the disjointed US payments and banking system). But without a single currency there will be a clear barrier to the flow of financial products, especially to the retail consumer. Transparency will also apply to the pricing of goods, affecting both the consumer, who is seeking to make effective comparisons, and the producer, who, in practice, has to deal at present with the difficult multicurrency pricing decisions (hence the dynamic benefits of EMU, as discussed).

Of course, if it is accepted that currency and monetary integration makes a significant difference to the wider aspects of economic integration, then it must also be accepted that integration will not be complete unless it extends outside these regions. Will this lead to a greater pressure to widen the reach of currency areas, to fix exchange rates between the major currencies? This brings us to the second area of discussion: global monetary developments.

Money and global integration

The increasing flows of private capital worldwide have been, and continue to be, a powerful force behind the globalization of finance and the interconnection between economies and economic policy. Freer capital flows since 1971 led to the growth in the global FX market. The steady removal of other capital controls have helped to turn the offshore euromarket into a more global integrated market, in part by eliminating the need for an offshore market as such. In the 1960s and early 1970s, exchange controls separated the euromarket's offshore pool of money from certain domestic markets, but now that the barriers have gone this offshore pool is interlinked with all major domestic markets. Therefore, in theory, the euromarket would not have to be developed further today, although a pool of expertise, such as that in the FX market, would still have to exist.

There are four aspects of this part of the monetary integration story that are worth dwelling upon: the trend towards economic and monetary policy coordination, especially exchange-rate management; the impact of the massive flows of Japanese finance; the importance of the boom in direct foreign investment; and the debate among economists following the publication of evidence which seemed to contradict the idea that capital markets were becoming more integrated, despite globalization.

Economic and monetary policy coordination
International economic policy coordination has never really gone away, but the attitude to such coordination and the respective responsibilities of each nation have altered. In the aftermath of the collapse of Bretton Woods, and the failure to develop any coherent post-Bretton Woods structure, there was perhaps a decade of non-coordination, with the markets being left to lead the way. That first period was, at the same time, one of rising inflation, divergent policies and divergent reactions to the oil crisis and recession. A shift occurred at the Bremen summit of 1978, when Germany agreed to played the locomotive role to lead coordinated recovery. The further rise in inflation and the twists and turns of US policy over the next five years and even the setting-up of the EMS did little for the image of coordination, offering neither success in terms of stability or of sustainable growth nor, in the view of policymakers, any other tangible benefits. Meanwhile, the fading hegemon, the United States, was entering a new period of benign neglect of its currency and the novelty of 'Reaganomics' and the supply-side revolution.

The next watershed was reached in 1985, when the United States agreed once again to intervene on currency markets, and, in a parallel development, the EMS began to find its feet. At the same time the problem of the twin deficits and global imbalances between industrial nations was occupying policymakers' minds, as was the awkward issue of the LDC debt crisis. In most respects we are still in this phase: central banks still aim to keep the dollar at competitive levels; and coordination is still on the agenda, albeit in rather a fragile fashion. It is by no means clear either that the will to alter domestic policy to suit the common global strategy is there or that, should the growth paths of Germany and the United States diverge, the cooperative approach will be able to survive. The most concrete progress towards more global cooperation has been the steady convergence within the EC to provide for a third leg, but even that has yet to be consolidated.

It would seem to be too early to talk of a global currency; indeed, to envisage it today would probably bring the end-of-geography story into disrepute. There are still too many differences among economies to allow such a system, remembering that a system on the Bretton Woods model is no longer possible unless the clock is turned back and exchange controls imposed all round. The end of geography precludes such a scenario, and thus fixed rates would require integration by desire not by force.

The Japanese wall of money
A particular phenomenon in recent years has been the flow of money from Japan. It is important to distinguish between the outflow of funds which has financed Japanese direct investment worldwide – an investment that has often been designed to develop markets behind potential protectionist walls (i.e. recognizing the realities of trade geography) – and the flow of portfolio capital from Japan. The flow of portfolio capital has been important, not only in financing the US borrowing requirements, but also in supporting the international expansion of Japanese financial firms. The power of Japanese banks and securities firms has been in the financial resources at their disposal and the strong capital base they once enjoyed. Recent analysis suggests that while there is only limited evidence of a trade bloc emerging in Asia, led by Japan, there is stronger evidence of a yen bloc based on a more important role for Tokyo, another example of financial integration leading other forms of economic integration (see Frankel, 1991).

Two factors relevant to the end of geography have resulted from this Japanese flow of funds: the power gained by Japanese financial firms and the impact made by Japanese ownership of assets in other countries, in the form of property, portfolio holdings and manufacturing capacity. The latter factor is likely to be the most important in the long term, since the former is likely to decline if the Japanese current account closes in the next few years (although it is showing signs of widening again now!). This direct-investment story need not, however, be confined to the Japanese aspects.

The boom in direct foreign investment

The boom in direct foreign investment raises many end-of-geography issues. Perhaps most significant is the impact that it has on the cross-border ownership of companies, which also occurs through international portfolio investment. The change in ownership also helps to undermine the identity between the external balance-of-payments accounts (current and capital accounts) and the national interest. It is this aspect that has attracted special attention in recent analyses (see Julius, 1990, 1991, and Turner, 1991).

Ownership issues have a particular impact on the financial sector, in which there are significant cross-shareholdings within countries among companies and financial institutions. German banks have strong influence over German companies, and as a result it is difficult to see how foreign (including other European) firms can compete on a level playing-field in the German market. In theory, eventually it would be permissible to extend such links to include non-German banks, although whether it will happen in practice is questionable. In the United States, meanwhile, one of the most powerful populist calls against strong links between companies and banks (not, it is important to note, argued in this way by *all* who wish to keep commerce and banking separate) is, 'Do you want Honda to own Citibank?', which is seen as even worse, presumably, than Honda owning General Motors.

From the point of view of the trend towards integration, it might seem that direct foreign investment is significantly different from portfolio investment or banking flows, given the higher ownership levels involved and the higher degree of direct foreign investor control. Certainly in the political arena this is plausible, as the setting-up of a foreign-owned manufacturing company has a visibility that is not so readily apparent in other fields: even foreign ownership of the Rockefeller Center in New York is not so immediately visible to the naked eye. Yet, in the end-of-geography context, there may not be such a difference between the types of flows. First, portfolio flows are also the stuff of takeovers (and restrictions on such flows through complicated share-ownership restrictions, as practised in Switzerland, for example, are just as critical as for direct investment flows). Second, portfolio flows and banking flows may be even more volatile and reversible (and there is only one thing worse than an inflow of foreign capital, and that is an outflow of that money at a later date!). Third, portfolio capital, in practice, is likely to represent a much less transparent flow. Each company can assess the nationality of its share ownership, but it is by no means readily visible. The only consolation is that such ownership is diversified, and so limits the power of any one owner (until certain visible reporting levels are reached, when it does become an issue, as was the case with the Kuwaiti ownership of more than 15% of BP). Portfolio flows play their part also in facilitating particular economic policies and strategies (such as running large current imbalances and budget deficits), and thus can have a long-lasting effect on the world economy. And portfolio investment obviously helps to integrate stock markets and the cross-border ownership of firms, perhaps more discreetly transferring ownership.

In the final analysis, the fungibility of money means that the definition of the types of flows, for the policymaker, should not be of great importance. As Turner points out, the importance of financial flows in the free capital movements of today represents a striking departure from the pattern of international capital flows in the late nineteenth century, the other great period of free-flowing global capital, when the bulk went into railways and other real assets. In terms of the profitability or rate of return of investment, there is probably little distinction between flows to apparent, real or financial assets. Perhaps the main distinction comes when there are real goods and products that can be observed, activities that can be policed. Local content can be applied somewhat more readily to car production than to, say, a financial service. Yet, even those differences soon disappear: financial services depend upon technology, and local content rules can be applied (as in Brazil) that directly affect the inflow of foreign financial expertise and services.

Investment, savings and the cost of capital
The economics profession was somewhat surprised by the results of an analysis made by Feldstein and Horioka (1980), which observed that, despite all the trends towards internationalization, most savings went into domestic investment, that there was a close correlation between domestic savings and investment. In other words, capital mobility was low. This conclusion does not fit the end-of-geography story. However, recent research and trends seem to lead to the opposite conclusion, that there is indeed a high degree of capital mobility (see Cooper, S., 1991, for a useful dicussion of the latest work on capital mobility). This is

doubly helpful, since not only does it remove the awkward evidence of low capital mobility but it also suggests that there has been a radical shift towards capital mobility in the past decade, which of course fits with the other evidence that can be seen from the removal of exchange controls across the globe. In other words, the essence of the end-of-geography story is new! Of course, this also accords with Henderson's observation that, despite the slow pace of integration in the real economy, the pace of integration is fast in finance.

However, two further questions need to be addressed. First, will the high level of capital mobility, a phenomenon largely associated with the relaxation of controls in the 1980s, revert to a more mundane pattern after the portfolio adjustment has taken place? And, second, what effect does this capital mobility, especially if it is to be sustained, have on the real economy? Will it accelerate integration in other fields, or will the end of geography remain a finance phenomenon while the rest of the world integrates at a Henderson-observed pace (or will the financial integration stimulate just the sort of reaction that Henderson implies could accelerate the whole process)?

The resolution to the question of capital mobility should be revealed by analysis of the cost of capital across borders. In the past few years we have become mesmerized by the size of the net flows between countries, although it is clearly the gross flows that are important in terms of mobility. A large net flow that is a function of even larger and relatively free gross flows presents different policy questions than those of large flows that have to be induced, cajoled and do not flow through a relatively free market mechanism.

The problem is that measurement of the cost of capital across borders is not easy. The big differences are those that still exist between equity markets. Capital markets, on the other hand, are clearly well-integrated, at least for the major borrowers. Interest-rate differences that used to prevail between euromarket rates and domestic rates have all but disappeared. The cost of money is equalizing at least for the larger wholesale borrowers and is likely, at least in part, to represent one of the differences between the integration at a wholesale level and that at retail level, retail markets still being subject to local differences (hence the attraction of the single market as a way to reduce the cost of financial services in the retail sector in the EC). If local borrowers still find some pricing differences, that is a function of their size rather than the lack of globalness of the market (in the same way that small businesses and local businesses in economies will sometimes find differential costs in capital). Raising money on equity markets, however, is still different from country to country. As already discussed, equity markets and companies continue to show more differential characteristics than currencies and monetary instruments. In other words, the overall cost of capital is not yet wholly equalized, since equity markets retain differences.

Other integration issues

There are three other important integration and globalization issues on the agenda which must at least be referred to, if only briefly: trade integration, including the development of trade blocs of one sort or another, and the efforts towards a free-trade regime in services (GATS); the integration of developing countries into the world economy; and the disintegration of certain federations, notably the USSR, Yugoslavia and the Comecon bloc.

Trade integration

The most sceptical readers of this study are likely to be trade economists. As Henderson points out, trade regimes are becoming less liberal. The efforts to eliminate tariff barriers have been offset by the addition of non-tariff barriers, including the whole host of trade-distorting measures, such as voluntary restrictions on exports. In other words, the end-of-geography challenge presented by the liberalization of trade was met by a strong geographical counter-action, ensuring that each old barrier was replaced in another way. Furthermore, the whole negotiating structure to ensure free trade, the GATT, is based on the concept of separate nation-states, each bargaining for their national interest. This has no place in the end-of-geography world and is as outdated as balance-of-trade statistics. But it exists. Will the end of geography in finance go the same way as trade in goods? Do the efforts to put trade in services, investment and finance through the negotiations threaten our brave new world?

There are two hopeful signs. First, the fungible nature of money does allow finance to flow more easily across borders. Henderson notes the faster progress of finance in this regard. With or without the GATS, wholesale markets will continue to integrate. Perhaps at the retail level, the nation-state will be able to slow the process much more, if it so desires, and protectionism with respect to retail payments systems will continue to threaten the consumer of financial services. Second, the shift from the nation-state to the trade bloc, despite the risks, is being driven in part by end-of-geography forces. This conclusion rests on the assumption that the expansion of organizations from the national to the regional stage is a precursor of the movement from the regional to a more global stage. Europe is integrating on a regional basis because the separation into individual nations no longer makes sense. Of course, there is a strong effort to rebuild the national powerbase at the regional level, which in the extreme could mean Fortress Europe. But the very diversity of the region makes it more difficult to develop a centralized structure for the region: hence a federalist structure is the most likely. In a situation in which the centre does forge an unholy alliance of interests, the consequences can be serious, as the Common Agricultural Policy shows, and then the regional structure is at its worst (and hence becomes the basis of interregional dispute). Thus, despite the importance of the current GATS talks, a good end-of-geographer should not be too influenced by whether they succeed or fail. Interestingly, even those examining the new structure of trade have a strong focus on the 'nation'. For example, Michael Porter's *The Competitive Advantage of Nations* (1990) shows how competitiveness depends on clusters of skills within economies. The implication of his book is that it is the components of nations that are in competition, not nations *per se*.

LDC integration

The reader from developing countries will, in common with the trade economist, have reason to feel short-changed by this study. Much of the discussion focuses on the sharp end of change, the hi-tech financial world of the late twentieth century, far removed from many developing-country experiences. The very nature of development implies a significant lag on events in the rich economies. Yet the developing world comes into the story in several important ways.

In the early 1970s, the developing countries burst onto the international financial scene: first, in 1971–3 as newly rich commodity exporters; second, in 1974 as cash-starved oil importers; and third, in 1974, a different group, as cash-rich oil exporters. The LDCs accounted for more than 40% of syndicated euroloans in the world's powerful euromarket, and oil states were the single largest group of depositors. Developing countries were indeed in the centre of the world's most advanced type of end-of-geography global marketplace.

The sudden reversal of this trend in the early 1980s, when the debt crisis erupted, will suggest to many that the experience of the 1970s was all a historical accident, an aberration that will eventually fade from memory like a bad dream – an aberration, that is, in terms of the business of banks making longer-term balance-of-payments loans (see O'Brien, 1985). But, despite the permanent scar that the 1970s (often known as the 'lost decade') left on many banks' balance sheets and on many developing nations, this period of activity undoubtedly created a closer bond between the LDCs and the rest of the world. First, some of the borrowers are graduating to almost developed-economy status, notably South Korea and Taiwan (mainly a depositor), while other Asian economies, such as Indonesia, are developing more sophisticated financial systems. Second, the banking industry's knowledge of developing economies is far superior to that which it had in the 1960s, even if some of the contacts have been developed more around the rescheduling table than in more positive arenas. The bond will not be wholly eliminated, despite many banks reducing their international activities in LDCs. Third, at times the United States and other countries have taken into account the impact of their monetary policies on the LDCs. Even if the connection was made for the more self-interested reason of wanting to protect banks that had made loans to LDCs, the connection between dollar interest rates and LDC prosperity was established. And, fourth, many banks still have extensive networks in LDCs: trade finance and correspondent banking, for example, still go on.

None the less there is still a concern that LDCs will remain marginalized, that the free flow of investment capital will somehow bypass them, and indeed that, in a free-flowing competitive world, the flows will go to other areas, such as Eastern Europe. This is not the place to become embroiled in the confusing debate over the so-called global savings shortage (a much exaggerated phenomenon). The reality is that the barriers to the flow of capital to the LDCs lie not in the supply conditions but in the economic conditions of the developing economies. It is clearly not in the interest of LDCs to start large borrowings from the global bond or credit markets to finance their balance of payments, although over time there is no reason why LDC companies should not tap all markets, dependent on their own access to foreign currency. The biggest barrier is of course the weakness of LDC currencies, their relative lack of convertibility, so that there is a very definite country risk associated with currency and transfers. In other words, until the currencies of the LDCs are sounder, and until their economies are left to live with international pressures and governments become willing to remove capital controls, there will remain a distinct, geographical country risk for lenders and investors to consider.

The longer-term integration depends more on financial deepening in the LDCs than on the flow of international capital to them. Many economic problems stem from insufficient domestic savings, inadequate investment opportunities at home and the flight of capital from uncertain economic prospects. The development of new technology has enabled LDCs to instal sophisticated information and banking systems. At the early stage of development, the foreign banks in an LDC have a distinct competitive advantage, but the transfer of knowledge is relatively swift in this service and, where the LDC permits it, this transfer (usually IT) can soon make the local provider of services very competitive. Indeed, the investment in technology now makes it easier and quicker to transfer money across Brazil than across the United Kingdom, and certainly than across Europe. To some extent, of course, the links have made capital flight even easier: but that is not relevant to this study.

In the securities markets, the interest in emerging stock markets undoubtedly represents the beginnings of a more permanent flow of longer-term risk capital to developing countries, even if the very nature of these new stock markets means volatility, extraordinary price swings and often insufficient liquidity at times of crisis. Portfolio flows into LDC companies should be able to play a major role, alongside the most direct forms of foreign investment.

Finally, the integration of the LDCs' financial markets into global markets is being actively pursued. The capital adequacy standards are providing one focus for the question of whether LDC banks will 'join the club'. If LDC banks wish to be active internationally there will be pressure to conform. At the same time, access to developing country banking and other financial systems is being actively sought: naturally the host LDCs are cautious as to the impact that more competition will have on their own financial institutions, and most LDC financial markets are still subject to considerable local protection of one form or another, including interest-rate regulation. Directed lending is a classic way of both managing many LDCs' local capital formation and providing advantages to domestic firms.

Disintegration

The final end-of-geography aspect is also the newest: the sudden bursting upon the scene of the East bloc. Although in some cases the process is one of internal disintegration, the collapse of communism supports the thesis of this study rather than opposing it. The communist systems crumbled under the forces of economics (economies that were simply no longer competitive or even performing adequately by domestic standards) and under the pressures imposed by information. Glasnost, the freeing of information, led to perestroika, the liberalizing reform of economic activity. Alongside the internal disintegration, it is clear that the primary task of these countries is to rebuild their own economies, on a capitalist model (suitably tailored of course) and to integrate their economies with the rest of the world.

10

SUMMARY
AND CONCLUDING
RECOMMENDATIONS

This paper has sped across many subjects and has raised many issues without even attempting the further analytical task of gauging the extent of change. I make no apology for the attempt to cover such a wide canvas, only for the sketchiness with which many aspects have been treated. It is now time to try to make some coordinated sense of the complicated picture and to set out a few recommendations, however general. The chapter is divided into three parts: observations, prospects and the regulatory agenda.

Observations on the main categories of change
The kaleidoscope of multiple interconnected changes falls into nine main categories:

(1) *Barriers in finance have fallen and continue to fall at every level*, at national borders, between stock and other financial markets, between firms, between sectors of the financial services industry (e.g. insurance, banking, securities), between financial market cultures and systems, between previously separated regulatory areas.

(2) These changes are occurring at both *the retail and the wholesale level*: the wholesale markets, such as foreign exchange, show the most obvious progress, but the pace of change affecting the retail sector must not be underestimated, involving, as it does, new sales of retail financial services across borders as well as altering the domestic geography of retail finance.

(3) Parallel to the integration of finance is *the integration of economies* on a wider basis, ranging from the integration of economies at the macro level through to the cross-border integration of activity at the micro, company, level, for which production and sales facilities are developed on a multinational/global basis. The most obvious examples of this macro- and microeconomic integration are: the (regional) integration of economies, notably in Europe and North America, and less powerfully in Asia; the drift towards a more fixed exchange-rate regime, albeit very different from the Bretton Woods system, which depended heavily on intervention, controls and strong national barriers; the boom in direct foreign investment and the greater international ownership of firms, so that ownership of the firm no longer tallies with national geographies.

However, this economic integration is proceeding at a slower pace than the integration of finance, and, in the arena of world trade, we should not dismiss the drift towards a less-free-trading system. What is clear is that this integration of economies depends as much on the actions of the firm (and the so-called dynamic effects that are expected to power the EC 1992 effort) as on the efforts of governments to coordinate, cooperate and integrate.

(4) For the parallel integration of finance and economies more generally, *the connecting rod is the massive and freer flow of capital worldwide*. Exchange rates can no longer be run by government intervention: their only real power is through the macroeconomic levers that can still be pulled, affecting domestic economies in the short to medium run. The market punishes mistakes of policy very quickly. For the firm, the increasingly similar cost of capital worldwide reflects the integration of capital markets: a global price of capital. In recent years, the evidence of this free flow of capital has been the boom in international lending; of course, in a perfectly integrated market, where the cost of capital is the same, there do not even have to be large amounts of capital moving across borders, flowing between pools of capital (see Bryant), as long as the price is efficiently arbitraged through flows of money at the margin.

(5) The third parallel process of integration is occurring at the *political* level. The EC process is driven by the long-running political desire to prevent conflict, even though it has also to be powered by forces for economic integration. The disintegration of the Soviet Union and the collapse of East/West physical and ideological barriers likewise involve both political and economic change; glasnost and

perestroika are both end-of-geography forces. The disintegration of the existing order in the former communist world reflects the effort to integrate these hitherto isolated economies into the Western trading and economic system, requiring an integration of ideas as well as of economic activity.

Meanwhile, it is worth stressing that political integration means, quite literally, the integration of people(s). If the free movement of capital is indicative of the flow of economic activity across borders, it is the freer flow of people (labour) across borders that is the true measure and most powerful manifestation of political integration, whether from East Germany to West Germany or from Mexico to the United States. But even today labour is less mobile than capital. Thus labour needs capital (and policy should encourage free capital flows), but that capital will flow in the direction of labour resources only if the labour is productive. Hence the competition among nations depends on effective investment in human resources. Capital will not flow towards an uneducated, skill-deficient labour resource, and such a resource also has a diminished mobility (a vicious circle to be in, as Reich stresses).

(6) The introduction of *new information technology* in finance is both an obvious observable change and a powerful force for other changes in finance, as well as in almost every other walk of life. As has already been discussed at some length, new communications and new computer technologies are together altering the dimensions of markets, the relative importance of location and the organization of firms, and destroying those barriers around markets that hitherto have been synonymous with specific geographical coordinates. Computerization powers the innovations in techniques that, with the force of rapid communications networks, make for an unstoppable combination. Securitization is driven by the IT revolution, and each new payments system introduces an almost new form of money as a transactions vehicle.

The IT revolution is also irreversible, although the full impact of new IT does require massive investment on the part of the service provider and its acceptance on the part of the user. The invention of a new piece of software or hardware does not guarantee its use or introduction. This is not helped by the pace of innovation, which gives each new invention a potentially short shelf-life: even the much vaunted fax machine, with its momentous impact so many years after its actual invention may soon be superseded by electronic mail and other computer-based services.

(7) Alongside the IT revolution is *the regulatory revolution*, based on the triple agenda of change in the marketplaces of Europe, the United

States and Japan. Each agenda is determined by strong domestic forces and tends to be decided by domestic interests. Yet each domestic debate is increasingly influenced by external pressures. Thirteen items, deemed to be of global importance, have been identified on the regulatory agenda, the primary focus of this study's recommendations.

Regulatory change is here to stay but increasingly incorporates reregulation as well as deregulation. Yet the persistent trend is likely to favour more open markets, despite efforts to protect existing boundaries (i.e. efforts to combat and resist the end of geography). Major problems will undoubtedly occur when markets prove to be incompatible, when 'systemic friction' occurs. Like the personal computer world, however, the trend will be towards establishing industry standards, whether in terms of the dealing and communications systems now rivalling themselves in the PC and telecommunications market or in terms of the financial structures which still show major differences in approach (i.e. 'universal' banking versus the US segmented model). Ultimately, the end-of-geography challenge is a challenge to regulators.

(8) The most worrying aspect of the 1990s for many observers is the apparent *'financial fragility' of markets*. Those worries have been exacerbated by the fallout after Big Bang, the costs of the LDC debt crisis, the S&Ls crisis in the United States, problems in the US insurance industry from junk bond investments, property price-falls in major markets, the failure of the banking supervisors to prevent the collapse of BCCI, and the worries engendered by the stock market crashes of 1987 and 1989. In 1982, international finance started to deal with the LDC debt problem, the legacy of the boom of the 1970s. In the early 1990s, the markets are dealing with many legacies of the boom in innovation of the 1980s.

(9) Finally, efforts are being made to develop *more global rules* and *more global cooperation*. In the macroeconomic context, such efforts have developed in the arena of exchange rates, led by the Group of Seven, in trade in goods and services, notably the efforts to widen the scope of the GATT negotiations, as well more 'global' governance at the regional level in the EC, the laboratory test-case for integration in finance, economics and politics. In the financial marketplace, the trend towards some sort of global governance is best represented by the efforts of bank supervisors under the aegis of the Bank for International Settlements in Basle to impose common minimum capital requirements on banks, and, in conjunction with supervisors and regulators in other financial sectors (securities and insurance), to integrate and coordinate the supervision of banking, securities markets and insurance.

The end of geography: prospects and challenges

The glorious end-of-geography prospect for the close of this century is the emergence of a seamless global financial market, bringing back memories (for those with long memories) of the free-capital era of the late nineteenth century. Barriers will be gone, service will be global, the world economy will benefit and so too, presumably, will the customer, being offered 'global choice'.

For many observers this seamless prospect is somewhat utopian, at least in terms of its attainability as opposed to desirability. A more sober look at the crystal ball suggests a rather bumpy road towards seamlessness: intense competition among financial firms, with major bankruptcies, forced mergers followed by massive shakeouts, crises for customers and producers alike, repeated losses from overambitious investment in new technologies, financial crises leading to the socialization of losses (à la S&Ls) and seemingly intractable problems in reconciling the fundamental differences between contrasting financial systems.

Emerging from this discouraging scenario may be a reaction against end-of-geography trends on two counts: policymakers could be increasingly called upon to protect not only the national interest but also that of the consumer. 'Rampant' international competition would be seen as a threat to them both and, with plenty of scope for raising fears of financial fragility, the protectionist case would be able to use fears of systemic risk to bolster its case. Such a protectionist reaction against the end-of-geography suggests a nightmare prospect where well-intentioned efforts to ensure utopia through intervention (in order to avert systemic risks) – all in the interests of protecting the consumer and ensuring fair competition and level playing-fields – strangles the world financial system with global rules, distorting firms' structures, stifling innovation and eventually adding costs to the public purse. Classic warning signs can be seen in the difficulties faced by the United Kingdom in establishing workable and cost-effective rules for the City of London (as with the Financial Services Act, 1986); in the S&Ls débâcle, a long-forecast disaster combining moral hazard (i.e. where insurance can encourage risky behaviour) with the costs of partial deregulation; and in the on-going debate over capital adequacy, as regards both its efficacy for banks and its extension to the rest of the financial services industry.

Fungibility of money versus the role of government

In practice, as we consider the theory and the realities of the end of geography, there are two counteracting forces which will struggle against each other. On one side, promoting integration, is the fungibility of money. Whatever efforts are made to maintain barriers in financial services or to define the role of money and the rules governing it, the job is almost impossible. Money is a creature of regulation: it is also adept at finding its way around regulation. Hence integration of capital markets has been able to move much faster than the integration of economies at large.

Counter to the freedom-of-money force is the fact that governments are the very embodiment of geography, representing the nation-state. The end of geography is, in many respects, all about the end or diminution of sovereignty. We are unlikely to witness governments presiding, actively and willingly, over their own demise. The preferred route is one of cooperation, through multilateral and bilateral negotiations and institutions whose members are governments and nations, who represent and uphold the sovereignty of nations. It is very hard to mix this structure with markets that know no such boundaries. In other words, governments and policymakers must be expected to defend geography, unless they can perceive an alternative geography.

There is also a key difference between the public policymaker and the market participants in their respective attitudes to the end of geography. The firm is far less wedded to the idea of geography. Ownership is more and more international and global, divorced from national definitions. Investors and borrowers think in international and global terms. If one marketplace can no longer provide a service or an attractive location to carry out transactions, then the firm will actively seek an alternative home. At the level of the firm, therefore, there are plenty of choices of geography. And this is especially true in finance, even though manufacturing also displays a tremendous ability to alter its geography to suit.

Kenichi Ohmae (1990), in his 'borderless world', hopes that 'government leaders will recognize that their role is to provide a steady and small hand, not to interfere'. If asked, many leaders and policymakers might agree today with that sentiment. But, as firms, regulators and marketplaces compete in the 1990s, it will be very hard for governments to avoid intervening to protect the consumer and the system. The consumer and the financial firms are likely to be the worst offenders in calling on governments to intervene when it suits, and to keep out at other times. It will be tempting for a government to take a nationalistic, populist line as it tries to determine where its priorities lie, especially when the very power of government, vis-à-vis other governments, is threatened. The siren calls put out by national champions, whether firms or markets, should be ignored.

The regulatory agenda and the end of geography

Regulators face an uphill task in keeping up with change in financial markets, and it would be naive to think that there are any simple recommendations that can be made to solve complex problems. But it would seem that there are a few broad choices that regulators must address in the coming years of change. Their top priorities are to protect the financial system from collapse and serious crisis, and to ensure that sound market practices are pursued. The consumer must be protected, the system must be safeguarded and the financial system itself must contribute to economic welfare. It is an axiom of the capitalist system that the process depends upon free and vigorous competition in the marketplace. The policy-choices emerge when these laudable objectives clash, when protecting the consumer threatens the system, when free competition threatens the system or when efforts to stabilize the system stultify the workings of the marketplace. The dilemmas emerge in the specific examples, such as deposit insurance, in trying to strengthen the capital adequacy of the securities industry. This study cannot hope to solve those dilemmas, but it may be possible to suggest how the balance of priorities for regulators and firms may be moving as the end of geography in finance develops over the decade.

For governments there are also the macroeconomic aspects to consider. The most important policy move in the past fifteen years has been the gradual relaxation of exchange controls across the OECD countries, and this has been a thread in the end-of-geography story, from the impetus given to the euromarkets by exchange controls in the 1960s, through to the liberalizing effect in the 1980s. Could exchange controls be reinstated? The fungibility of money suggests not, certainly not without considerable distortion of the marketplace, to the detriment of the system, the producer and the consumer. The cost of capital would certainly be distorted and resources allocated less efficiently. Money is just too fungible in the late twentieth century. If that is true, then the main macro-policy choice relating to the end of geography in finance (as opposed to the wider integration issues) would seem to be permanently in place, allowing the free movement of funds across borders. Any attempt to revert to a narrow, geographical approach is likely to be punished by the markets and ignored by fungible money.

The matrix shown in Figure 2 sets out the thirteen global challenges according to their level of difficulty and the importance of each issue, and in effect relating to their relevance to the march towards the end of geography. Since all these issues have been selected on grounds of their

Figure 2 A matrix of regulator choices showing difficulty of implementation and importance

	DIFFICULTY in implementing regulatory aims	
	Medium	*High*
IMPORTANCE as regulatory issue — *Medium*	Regulation of derivatives Restructuring exchanges Access to markets Data protection Money laundering	**Deposit insurance** **Capital adequacy** **Eliminating sectoral barriers**
High	**Clearance/settlements** **Accounting harmonization**	**PROTECTING CONSUMER** **FINANCE/COMMERCE LINKS** **COORDINATION OF REGULATION/SUPERVISION**

global relevance, all are ranked as being at least of medium importance. The easy tasks, of lesser importance, may be left aside.

While none of these issues are so self-contained as to be easily placed in a single box, the aim of the matrix is both to give some idea of regulatory priorities and to assess the extent of the barriers en route to the end of geography. Issues are listed in terms of their importance as regulatory goals vis-à-vis improving the workings of the international financial markets: e.g. protecting the consumer or improving the clearance/settlements system are seen as more important than writing data protection laws. Issues also are listed in terms of the difficulty in getting the regulations in place: for example, deposit insurance systems, so complicated by moral hazard issues, probably present a tougher challenge than negotiating access to markets. The matrix also 'works' with respect to the end of geography: in the lower right-hand box are the regulatory issues which not only perhaps represent the greatest obstacles to achieving globally integrated, seamless markets (i.e. high on the 'difficulty' scale), but also are the most important issues needing to be solved in order to achieve integrated markets.

Medium importance/medium difficulty

To begin with the five challenges ranked 'medium' in terms of both difficulty and importance: restructuring stock exchanges and the regulation of derivative markets are closely related. These are ranked as being of medium difficulty, not to minimize the seemingly intractable battles that exchanges have been engaged in (e.g. the long-running discussions as to whether the trading of commodity futures should be regulated by the futures regulators or the commodity regulators), but because these disputes are likely to be settled over time as the links between the markets develop and as their interaction becomes more familiar. The restructuring of the stock exchanges, however hard (as the debate in Europe reveals), seems to be moving inexorably towards more interlinked trading networks, where more stocks trade on more exchanges and where attempts to preserve the existing geography can only delay, not prevent, change. Eventually local exchanges will find that their ability to control trading in the more local companies will prevail, whereas the stocks of international companies will be traded more widely. Undermining the efforts of any exchange to preserve its historic position is the fact that its members, ultimately, will migrate to the most profitable market, with few geographical loyalties.

Also in this medium/medium category is access to markets. Whenever firms have sought to enter other markets, in other countries or other sectors, the debate is primarily about market share and protecting the incumbent players. It is more and more difficult to deny firms access to markets in one form or another or, in the end-of-geography context, to prevent the financial service from being provided despite barriers. Hence the debate becomes one of reciprocity, the jargon for horse-trading. Thus the United Kingdom, long the champion of open markets, has not been averse to using the reciprocity arguments to gain access for British firms in Japan, gentle 'crowbar' tactics. In the EC, the single market already has acceded on the issue of access, the regulatory emphasis shifting towards policing those who do have easy access to markets through their EC passport.

Should money laundering or data protection really be ranked as being of less than highest importance? The reasons for their medium/medium ranking are as follows: money laundering is clearly a high priority in other arenas, notably in the war against drugs – a war that has proved far more effective in breaking down the barriers to financial account secrecy than the war against tax evasion or the pursuit of the booty of dictators. Its high importance in that context is indisputable. But, in the context of the regulatory aim to protect the financial system and the consumer of financial services, money laundering would not seem to be of the highest priority (despite the fact that the collapse of BCCI was linked to its widespread practice). Indeed, it might not be going too far to suggest that money laundering, with respect to protecting the soundness of the system and the consumer, is of low importance. As to difficulty, it is ranked medium: although there has been some success in strengthening rules to combat money laundering, money's fungibility makes this an uphill task (which might even warrant a high-difficulty ranking). Moreover, tracing the flow of money through bank accounts worldwide is likely to become even more difficult as more financial services are offered globally, not to mention an increase in the ways in which monies can be switched into other assets to interrupt the paper trail. The efforts will undoubtedly continue while the drug problem persists.

Data protection likewise would appear to be of medium importance and of medium difficulty to solve: it is important, like money-laundering legislation, with respect to other political and social aims, but not so directly important vis-à-vis the regulation of financial markets. Indeed, if excessive data protection laws are put into place they could hamper the movement of money and limit the scope of financial services. Thus there is a possibility that regulatory change in this area could, almost inadvertently, prove to be a more significant obstacle to the end of geography than the matrix suggests. The issue has of course come to prominence as a result of the revolution in IT, making it easier to process and communicate sensitive credit and other information

High importance/medium difficulty

Two relatively similar issues are ranked high in importance and medium in difficulty: improving clearance and settlements systems, and harmonizing accountancy standards. Although those engaged in either activity will question any ranking below high on the difficulty scale, the main strategy is one of continuing to draw up and refine effective rules that define positions between participants, where they rest and what happens in the case of crisis. So far, the relative pace of progress in pursuing the various standards suggested under the aegis of the Group of Thirty and various working-groups would seem to testify to the medium-difficulty ranking.

Accountancy standards are of course hard to harmonize and efforts to do so are moving only slowly. However, this would seem to be more a matter of continuous refinement and negotiation, accounting being more of a mathematical exercise than a social science issue. There is, however, no question that efforts to harmonize accountancy standards and to solve the possible systemic risks inherent in the clearance/settlements area are of the highest importance and are essential to achieving well-integrated markets: imprecise rules on settlements can cause massive losses and chain collapses in the markets, while differences in accounting practices (and standards) can make a mockery of efforts to standardize other aspects of the market, such as capital adequacy. Neither task will ever be finished, but with method and coordination it would seem that considerable progress can be made.

.

Medium importance/high difficulty

The three issues in this category have been subject to considerable debate in recent years, as barriers have been taken down, as capital adequacy rules have been put into place for international banks, and as the deposit insurance costs have risen in the United States and have been discussed more actively in Europe after the BCCI collapse. The reduction of sectoral barriers is ranked in the matrix as being of considerable difficulty, since the whole structure of many financial markets is built around long-standing financial industry arrangements. Removal of Glass-Steagall has been under consideration for at least a dozen years, yet it is being eroded only slowly. External pressures do accelerate the process (i.e. end of geography is a factor here), but even so, as discussed, the agenda is often domestic. The glacial pace of change is testimony to the difficulty of change, with two factors tending to slow the pace: first, each problem in the market dissuades a significant part of the legislature from granting new or broader powers to those who are already not performing their present tasks properly; and, second, the interest groups in each market are often themselves as much threatened by change as welcoming it.

The difficult process moves in fits and starts. For the national regulators (or sub-national regulators) the urgency of the issue is limited by the overriding priority to safeguard the system (and change is rarely seen as the way to safeguard systems). Unless crisis occurs, the tendency is towards preserving existing systems, on the 'if it ain't broke, don't fix it' principle. Ultimately it must be important for the financial system to adapt, but in the immediate future the rapid removal of barriers is not seen as being of top priority. Each nation has built its own system, based on deliberate design and accidents of history. No nation can boast a system that, in its entirety, is clearly superior to any other system. Thus it is hard to say that change in any one nation is imperative. Whether the systems can work alongside each other in an end-of-geography world is a more difficult issue, and relates more widely to the links between finance and commerce (discussed below).

Capital adequacy rules are designed to protect the system, to ensure that the players have adequate capital to support their business and to act as a resource for coping with risks. Capital adequacy rules and deposit insurance are ranked as being of medium importance, since they are both a means to an end. Neither approach is perfect, but both are very difficult to impose: capital adequacy is ultimately of limited value, but at least when a bank has run out of capital the regulators can declare it insolvent. Yet we have seen that the rule is often applied too late, and that in the worst cases even 8% capital is insufficient to support a failed institution. On a global basis it is very hard to design a system of capital ratios that can be fair to all players. It seems likely that, after a while, a fresh approach to capital adequacy will be taken, on the grounds that the present effort will have served its purpose in encouraging banks to recapitalize. Once this improvement has taken place, much of the task should have been done (the process itself may result in considerable restructuring of banks that are inadequately capitalized). However, the process should not be allowed to fail for fear of nebulous dangers, such as global savings shortages: relaxing rules to boost credit is hardly a sound recipe for the world economy and its financing. A great deal of work will continue to be done in terms of position risk, interest-rate risks, and ensuring that firms are adequately protected for playing in new markets where risks are greater, such as options markets. But defining capital rules for sectors outside banking will be an even more difficult task.

Deposit insurance is also a means to an end. It has yet to be decided how to approach deposit insurance throughout the EC, but it looks more and more likely that protection levels will have to be coordinated and pressure put on home banks to provide the cover for losses. This will be an example where the regulatory task will be to link who pays with who should be protected. It is a case of no regulation without responsibility for the costs. In the United States, deposit insurance has been high on the agenda after a large number of failures among savings and loans have resulted in high cost to the public purse, raising the question of whether even large depositors ought to continue to be bailed out. Any issue involving moral hazard is inevitably complex, making deposit insurance a potentially high-difficulty candidate. However, it would seem that the solution will lie in restating and tightening-up on its use and abuse, limiting the cost to the exchequer in the future. Getting deposit insurance and capital adequacy right is difficult, ostensibly a high barrier to the end of geography and integration. But even with mixed success in finding truly satisfactory solutions, neither issue is likely seriously to arrest progress towards integration.

High importance/high difficulty

The remaining three issues in the matrix emerge as high-priority issues and perhaps the most likely to be intractable. It is their complexity and far-reaching implications that lead to this ranking. Each one has a special aspect that makes them of great importance. In the long run, if progress is limited, then integration (the end of geography) is likely to be severely restricted. Coordination of regulation and supervision is horrendously complex on a global basis, which includes the regulation of all financial sectors and markets. The need for more coordination and understanding on a global basis could hardly be greater. The protection of the consumer has a direct link to the political process, and governments, elected to defend voters, will find it extremely hard to get the balance right between ensuring that the consumer is offered safe goods at competitive prices and excessive drains on the exchequer. Finally, deciding on the appropriate links between finance and commerce is going to be a long-running saga, since the process will affect the very kernel of each country's economic activities. How companies are financed, how they are governed, how information about companies is shared and fed into the market and public arena, and how the efforts to safeguard the public purse from failures in either finance or commerce are all issues which lead us to this debate.

Coordination of regulation must be the oldest issue in the book, vis-à-vis globalization. Since 1973, banking supervisors have worked to coordinate the supervision of banks and their activities across frontiers. Much of the work had been done, but no sooner was it effected than the banking industry widened its remit, as sectors came together, and a further need emerged, requiring a similar task to be performed across a wider set of players, including the regulators of stock exchanges, of securities firms and of the insurance industry. The banking coordination process was relatively simple compared with these new tasks, mainly the diversity of the players. As a private-sector participant, it is difficult to suggest more coordination, since this could so easily mean more bureaucracy and more controls. Yet even the most libertarian free-market operators should ask whether it is a good thing that the world's financial system is regulated in such a haphazard way. Despite the efforts of the BIS, IOSCO and the OECD, we are a long way from having a full understanding of the interplay of financial markets and systems as the end of geography moves monies even faster. So far, the absence of coordination has been possible because either markets have been segmented (and regulated accordingly) or they have been of a universal nature, with a universal regulator. But the boxes have all been opened, and the cards shuffled.

It will be increasingly difficult to agree on the territorial boundaries of regulators. The current EC fashion to distinguish between home and host authorities will soon come up against the problem that home versus host is a geographical distinction that cannot be applied so easily to money. It is not an insuperable problem (i.e., everyone has to be somewhere and so will be deemed to be somewhere), but it offers many possibilities for responsibilities sliding into grey areas (BCCI, for example, despite reassurances that that could never happen again). Regulators will have to be even more open to negotiation on jurisdiction than in the past, across borders, within countries, between sectors and between exchanges. There is a case for trying to establish an overarching authority that can act as lead supervisor and regulator, preferably with a light touch.

In principle, *regulations to protect the consumer* of financial services should be relatively straightforward. Deposit insurance can be used to guarantee the money of at least the smaller depositors; licensing of firms controls their access to the consumer market; and those handling consumers' savings in the form of mutual funds, unit trusts and various collective savings instruments can be regulated for their soundness. Continued vigilance against fraud is necessary, as well as careful scrutiny of the selling techniques used to tempt the consumer to buy financial products and services.

The task of protecting the consumer is, however, becoming increasingly difficult as financial markets move towards end-of- geography conditions. First, in many economies the consumer is now taking more direct responsibility for investing his or her savings, as tax rates decline and new products, such as personal pensions and more savings vehicles, are launched. At the same time, privatization programmes seek to attract smaller investors into stock markets (as happened in the United Kingdom), where they have a limited access to the information needed to invest. Hence, over time, it is likely that the consumer investing in the stock market will entrust that investment to the professional investor.

The second complication comes from the internationalization of personal investments. With greater freedom to invest abroad, the consumer may also be investing in unfamiliar territories. For example, deposit insurance schemes are generally applicable only to the domestic market, yet more consumers will be looking at a wider geographical area for their savings, perhaps even investing with the same institution but crucially in other markets. Meanwhile, more foreign firms will be freer, especially in the EC, to sell services direct to the consumer.

The aim of policing sales practices is to ensure that the professional knows the needs of the consumer. When selling to the wholesale, professional, market, it is assumed that *caveat emptor* applies all the time, that the buyer is responsible for assessing the product on offer. In a more international market, 'knowing the customer' becomes more difficult when customs differ. In practice, this can be overcome by hiring local sales forces, but even these may be driven by foreign cultures and instructions.

The third aspect of difficulty comes from the political nature of protecting the consumer. Major losses to the consumer lead to strong pressure for those losses to be made good by the state, for the losses to be 'socialized'. Such a moral hazard cannot of course be allowed to take hold too easily. Undoubtedly there will be many who will lose deposit monies placed with the BCCI, not being fully aware of the risks and the limits of deposit insurance: the authorities will equally not wish to suggest that, whatever happens, the risk is not that of the consumer. Special cases can be withstood more easily: eventually, however, as the US deposit insurance scheme has shown, the process can go too far.

The risk is that the aim of protecting the consumer gets carried too far: the Gower Report (1985), which provided much of the intellectual support for the United Kingdom's Financial Services Act, explicitly ignored the cost of the regulatory structure, in part suggesting it was hard to quantify, in part suggesting that protecting the consumer was, in any case, an overriding objective. Eventually, of course, the consumer pays the price either in the quality of the service or in the choice of product offered. It is an extremely hard balance to get right, since both over-regulation and under-regulation can drive business to other centres (which then potentially makes it harder for the consumer to choose the right product). Thus, this issue is placed in the hard/hard category in view of the extreme difficulty of getting the balance right, the sheer range of views on what is or is not the correct balance, and the likelihood that, as markets integrate, the task will become more difficult, not easier.

The links between financial firms and non-financial businesses are of wide importance, since the effectiveness of the financial system itself has to be judged in the context of the health of the economy at large. Even a healthy banking system is not an end in itself: economic growth, prosperity and efficiency are the wider criteria for measuring success (without entering into the even wider issue of human welfare). The debate, however, does have some very specific aspects.

In the United States, the focus is on whether commercial firms should be allowed to own banks: the fear being that access to the Federal Reserve window and the lender of last resort facility could be corrupted. Even if the idea that banks are special can be adjusted to allow for intersectoral changes in the financial services industry, many feel that there should be a dividing line between finance and commerce.

The debate elsewhere is not pursued on these lines directly, but questions are coming from the other end of the spectrum. Is it appropriate that, through directorships and complex cross-ownership of shares, banks and companies should be so interdependent? Can these often discreet (if not actually secret) links be reconciled with the greater openness and flow of information consistent with the end of geography? The counter-argument has been to look at economic performance in Japan and Germany: companies have thrived, the banks have thrived and the economies have boomed. The Anglo-Saxon economies, in which finance and commerce have kept themselves separate (*de jure* or *de facto*), hardly have such a strong economic testimonial to support their case. But it would seem that time is running out for this aspect of the Japanese financial system and for this aspect of universal banking in Germany. As the German stock market, and that in Europe, develop, the clamour for a more open and equal flow of information about companies is likely to intensify. In Japan, the much-admired support of corporate asset values through interlinks has run into serious problems in the early 1990s. Japan's financial scandals are not just the result of excessive greed in the 1980s; they represent the shaking of the system, especially its closed nature. Corporate governance will be the hot topic for the 1990s.

Corporate governance is of course of key importance because it affects the running of the economy as a whole. If systems that have powered the most successful economies of the postwar period are under attack, then we do face a significant period of change. It will be difficult to shift from a closed way of sharing information, of determining credit flows, to an open system. Any compromise between open and closed systems is likely to be in favour of openness because of the fungibility of money. But the breaking of closed systems will be difficult, since it would be striking at one perceived reason for the success of German and Japanese firms: their access to long-term capital at low cost, without the threat of takeover.

The matrix is far from ideal and may obscure as well as clarify some issues. However, its most important contribution is in determining the issues for the lower right-hand box. In terms of the importance of regulatory issues and the difficulty in achieving regulatory aims, the matrix concludes that (1) protecting the consumer is of top priority and will be very diffi-cult as markets integrate; (2) altering the links between finance and com-merce, increasingly forced upon regulators as markets integrate, will be very tough to achieve, since such links lie at the heart of each economy's structure; and (3) coordinating regulation and super-vision of financial services, worldwide, is a Sisyphean task. With the possible exception of the elimination of sectoral barriers within the financial sector (being closely related to the finance/commerce issues) all the other issues somehow come a little lower on the scale, either because the problems can often be resolved through steady attention to detail or because as issues they strike less critically at fundamental differences between economies.

111

In terms of the end of geography, the issues in the lower right-hand box also seem to emerge from the fray. Protecting the consumer will become a potentially important bone of contention as integration starts to include the retail markets, and regulators and politicians could find nationalistic, protectionist pressures gaining strength. If the varying relationships between finance and commerce cannot be reconciled across different systems and economies, it is hard to see integration proceeding satisfactorily. And while the coordination of regulatory and supervisory structures has still so far to go, integration will be restricted and governed by the limitations of that coordination. Again, all the other issues in the matrix do have significant potential to upset the march towards the end of geography, but they either constitute barriers that will in any case be steadily eroded or are not in themselves so significant as to prevent effective integration.

Priorities for firms

Although the policy agenda applies primarily to the public sector, the end of geography presents just as many challenges to the private sector, especially the financial firm. Given that each firm will pursue its own strategy, it is difficult to recommend strategy. However, it may be worth speculating what sort of organizational changes will occur in coming years in financial services.

Ironically, although the global challenge is important, it is likely that many firms will be more preoccupied with their domestic position in the next few years. In the United States, the banks have entered a further period of restructuring, from the merger of money-centre banks, to the further strengthening of regional networks and the continued reduction in the number of small banks. Meanwhile the securities industry had still to recover from the collapse of business volume that came after the crash of 1987. Finally, the insurance industry has entered upon a period of change. In Europe a similar picture emerges, albeit with a more distinctive regional flavour rather than just focusing on the national scene. In Japan the increasingly intense competition for the domestic market among Japanese banks, securities houses and insurance companies has been given a further shake-up by the financial scandals.

Does this focus on 'one's own backyard' spell the end of the globalization era? How does the end of geography fit with US banks reducing their international networks and with the scaling-down of plans for securities firms after the pricking of the Big Bang bubbles? Unsurprisingly there is an 'end of geography' explanation, apart from the obvious point that both processes represent a degree of retrenchment after rapid expansion. As financial services markets integrate globally, more services can be provided by local firms (foreign firms bringing less value added) and better communications reduce the need for a physical presence globally. Production of services and a back-up can be provided from centres of excellence and distributed through sales networks. Economies of scale are enjoyed in production and servicing. Competitiveness will then depend on three things: the quality of the product or service itself, its price (of course) and the way the service is marketed. Hence the regulator of the consumer market spends a great deal of effort in monitoring both the sales forces and the way in which the customer is advised. As firms seek to differentiate their products, the emphasis is likely to be on the distribution and selling of what will often be very similar products.

All participants – governments and firms – will need to place as much attention on the globalization of retail finance as on that of wholesale finance. It is quite possible that the potential losses are greatest in retail integration, and, given the political impact of consumer losses, it is in this area that the temptation to combat the end of geography will be greatest. Firms will need to use alliances as temporary expediences. The bane of all joint ventures is the eventual change in priorities and powers of the partners: this will be even more apparent in a changing financial and economic environment. Thus any joint operation must look hard at the next stage, which could be a real merger, an early separation or a takeover.

Exchanges will need to develop networks and dilute their current identities. Exchange members should look to their future as members of networks, not of single exchanges. It is clear that these changes will be advanced most in the area of new products, as the different approach of the French MATIF towards Globex shows, compared with the more geographical approach of the Paris Bourse. The network and the associated clearing and settlements area will be the new territory to be defended.

Concluding remarks: focus on competition

The accepted aims of regulation are the protection of the system (which the players themselves have little incentive to do) and the protection of the consumer (the individual having little ability to protect himself). There is, however, a third aspect to regulation which may well emerge as the focus of global attention: competition policy. This is a hard policy to define in its own terms: competition is favoured as the route to achieve the other aims of protecting the system and protecting the consumer. A monopoly is easy to define; there is much greater difficulty in identifying what constitutes 'fair' competition. Concepts such as 'level playing-fields' sound sensible, but what does level really mean? Equality all round? Each marketplace has a good idea of what is acceptable practice, although this becomes harder to define as different market practices intermingle, when different groups have different ideas as to what warrants insider trading and whether such concepts are valid or not. As more banks and firms merge, competition in terms of the number of players may decline, though it is the intense competition that is forcing the mergers.

Ultimately every competition debate depends critically on which market is being considered. Is the market the national market, the regional market or the global market? Is the relevant definition of industry all of financial services or its constituent parts? As all the domestic debates show, the toughest competition in an industry that is restructuring comes from those outside the sector, whether banks entering the securities business or vice versa. Intrasectoral mergers thus develop to fight the 'outside' competition. Similar Europewide initiatives are taken to combat the outsider, and, although the single market has been pursued with the logical aim of establishing greater economies of scale for national firms within the EC, clearly the idea is to make these firms bigger and more competitive on the global stage. Yet the same economies of scale can be enjoyed by non-Europeans investing in Europe. Thus, in an end-of-geography context, the idea of promoting more competitive EC firms, with a European identity, is outdated. Calls to prevent a Trojan horse from entering the Community are based on the same doomed protectionist logic.

None the less, a substantial number of national and other identities will be retained. Firms may go global, but governments will not. The differences between sectors are likely to remain as long as each country preserves some of its special characteristics. It is impossible to expect governments not to champion and protect financial centres, which will still have an important role to play as agglomerations of product expertise, linked to more scattered sales networks in other centres. It is likely, however, that the most success will be gained by those who champion financial centres as open centres, attracting as much international business as possible, with little restriction on access and the main emphasis on sound market practices.

The world would be a dull place without diversity. Free trade will also ensure that, even if playing-fields become as level as English bowling-greens, product differentiation will provide for variety. The end of geography in finance may not be a particularly welcome concept: no sooner had seamless stockings been invented than designers started putting the seams back in. The end of geography will be resisted, sometimes with good reason. Financial services often depend on close personal contact, even if many routine tasks are better switched to the computer. But the fungibility of money, accelerated by the information revolution and encouraged by the fitful and often unreliable deregulation process, seems set to drive markets towards more openness and to lead to more conflicts between the systems and more competition among the firms and among those setting the rules. That competition cannot be unbridled: coordination of policies, better understanding of who is responsible for whom, is important to all regulators, producers and consumers interested in a healthy marketplace. Long-standing relationships between finance and commerce cannot be changed quickly without radically upsetting the macro and the micro economy. End of geography means competition. In the long run, 'competition among rules', however inelegant a phrase, is more likely to provide a flexible and manageable system than too much 'global governance'.

BIBLIOGRAPHY

The following works have been of great assistance in forming ideas on the end of geography, although only a limited number of them have been specifically cited in the text.

Amdahl Executive Institute (1991). 'Globalisation: the IT Challenge', report by Butler Cox plc.

Axilrod, Stephen (1990). *Interdependence of Capital Markets and Policy Implications*, Washington DC, Group of Thirty Occasional Papers, no. 32.

Baldwin, Richard E. (1991). 'On the microeconomics of EMU', in *European Economy*, special edition no. 1, Commission of the European Communities.

Bank for International Settlements (1986). *Recent Innovations in International Banking*, Basle, BIS, April.

Bank of England (1989). 'The market in foreign exchange in London', *Bank of England Quarterly Bulletin*, vol. 29, no. 4, November.

Benston, George J., et al. (eds.) (1986). *Perspectives on Safe and Sound Banking: Past, Present and Future*, Cambridge MA, The MIT Press for the American Bankers Association.

Bingham, T.R. Gavin (1991). 'The changing face of the global financial market', *Journal of International Securities Markets*, London, IFR Publishing Ltd, vol. 5, autumn.

Bryant, Ralph C. (1987). *International Financial Intermediation*, Washington DC, The Brookings Institution.

Commission of the European Communities (1990). 'One market, one money: an evaluation of the potential benefits and costs of forming an economic and monetary union', *European Economy*, no. 44, Brussels, October.

Cooper, Richard N. (1968). *The Economics of Interdependence*, New York, Columbia University Press for the Council on Foreign Relations.

Cooper, Shelley (1991). *Cross-border savings flows and capital mobility in the G7 economies*, Bank of England Discussion Papers, no. 54, March.

Corrigan, E. Gerald (1987). *Financial Market Structure: A Longer View*, Federal Reserve Bank of New York, January.

Cumming, Christine M., and Sweet, Lawrence M. (1978–8). 'Financial Structure of the G10 Countries: How does the United States Compare?' *Federal Reserve Bank of New York Quarterly Review*, winter.

Dale, Richard (1984). *The Regulation of International Banking*, Cambridge, Woodhead-Faulkner.

Davis, E. Philip (1991). 'International diversification of international investors', *Journal of International Securities Markets*, London, IFR Publishing Ltd, vol. 5, summer.

England, Catherine and Huertas, Thomas (1988). *The Financial Services Revolution*, Dordrecht, Kluwer Academic Publishers for the Cato Institute.

Feldstein, M., and Horioka, C. (1980). 'Domestic Saving and International Capital Flows', *Economic Journal*, 90.

Financial Regulation Report (various issues), Financial Times Business Information, monthly.

Frankel, Jeffrey A. (1989). *Quantifying International Capital Mobility in the 1980s*, National Bureau of Economic Research Working Paper Series, no. 2856, February.

Frankel, Jeffrey A. (1991). 'Is a yen bloc forming in Pacific Asia?', in Richard O'Brien (ed.), *Finance and the International Economy: 5*, Oxford, Oxford University Press.

Futures and Options World (1990). 'MATIF: the first five years', supplement.

Giovannini, Alberto, and Mayer, Colin (eds.) (1991). *European Financial Integration*, Cambridge, Cambridge University Press for the Centre for Economic Policy Research and Istituto Mobiliare Italiano.

Gower, L.C.B. (1984). *Review of Investor Protection*, London, HMSO.

Group of Thirty (1989). *Clearance and Settlements in the World's Securities Markets*, New York and London, March.

Grundfest, Joseph A. (1990). 'Internationalisation of the World's Securities Markets: Economic Causes and Regulatory Consequences', *Journal of Financial Services Research*, vol. 4, no. 4, December.

Haraf, William S., and Kushmeider, Rose Marie (eds.) (1988). *Restructuring Banking and Financial Services in America*, Washington DC, American Enterprise Institute for Public Policy Research.

Hayes, Samuel L. III, and Hubbard, Philip M. (1990). *Investment banking: A Tale of Three Cities*, Cambridge MA, Harvard Business School Press.

Henderson, David (1991). 'Peering Ahead: The 1990s in Historical Perspective', speech given to London seminar hosted by The Nikko Securities Co., (Europe) Ltd, April.

Hoekman, Bernard, and Sauvé, Pierre (1991). 'Integration and Interdependence: Information Technology and the Transformation of Financial Markets', part of an ATWATER Institute project on 'The Impact of Telecommunication and Data Services on Commercial Activity and Economic Development', mimeo.

International Financial Law Review (1991). 'The regulations governing insurance: an international guide', Euromoney publications, supplement, March.

International Monetary Fund (1991). *Determinants and Systemic Consequences of International Capital Flows*, Washington DC, IMF Research Department, March.

Jones, Geoffrey (ed.) (1990). *Banks as Multinationals*, London, Routledge.

Julius, DeAnne (1990). *Global Companies and Public Policy: The Growing Challenge of Foreign Direct Investment*, London, Royal Institute of International Affairs/Pinter.

Julius, DeAnne (1991). *Foreign Direct Investment: The Neglected Twin of Trade*, Washington DC, Group of Thirty Occasional Papers, no. 33.

Kaufman, Henry (1991). 'Capital Scarcity and Capital Allocation', address to International Monetary Conference, Osaka, Japan, June 4.

Key, Sydney J., and Scott, Hal S. (1991). *International Trade in Banking Services: A Conceptual Framework*, Washington DC, Group of Thirty Occasional Papers, no. 35.

Kindelberger, Charles P. (1984). *A Financial History of Western Europe*, London, Allen and Unwin.

Kindelberger, Charles P. (1987). *International Capital Movements*, Cambridge, Cambridge University Press.

Lamfalussy, Alexandre (1986). 'The World Economy: Major Policy Challenges for the Coming Years', address to the 25th Anniversary Conference of the Atlantic Institute for International Affairs in Brussels, November.

Leigh-Pemberton, Robin (1987). 'Ownership and control of UK banks', *Bank of England Quarterly Bulletin*, vol. 27, no. 4, November.

Maddison, Angus (1989). *The World Economy in the 20th Century*, Paris, OECD Development Centre Studies.

Meerschwam, David M. (1991). *Breaking Financial Boundaries*, Cambridge MA, Harvard Business School Press.

Mendelsohn, M.S. (1980). *Money on the Move: the Modern International Capital Market*, New York, McGraw-Hill Book Company.

Mitchell, Jeremy (1991). *Banker's Racket or Consumer Benefit?*, London, PSI Publishing for the Policy Studies Institute.

O'Brien, Richard (1985). 'Banking Perspectives on the Debt Crisis', *Oxford Review of Economic Policy*, vol. 2, no. 9, winter.

OECD (1988). 'Arrangements for the Regulation and Supervision of Securities Markets in OECD Countries', *Financial Market Trends*, no. 41, Paris, OECD, November.

OECD (1989). 'Recent Trends in Financial Regulation', *Financial Market Trends*, no. 44, Paris, OECD, Paris, October.

119

Bibliography

OECD (1990). *Liberalisation of Capital Movements and Financial Services in the OECD Area*, Paris, OECD.

OECD (1991), 'Automation of Securities Markets and Regulatory Implications', *Financial Market Trends*, no. 50, October.

OECD (1991). *Systemic Risks in Securities Markets*, Paris, OECD.

Ohmae, Kenichi (1990). *The Borderless World*, New York, Harper Business.

Ostry, Sylvia (1991). 'Beyond the Border: The New International Policy Arena', in *Strategic Industries in a Global Economy*, Paris, OECD.

Porter, Michael E. (1990). *The Competitive Advantage of Nations*, New York, The Free Press.

Price Waterhouse (1990). *Banking and Securities Regulation in Europe: A Survey of Senior Management Views*, February.

Quality of Markets Quarterly Review (various issues), London Stock Exchange.

Reich, Robert B. (1991). *The Work of Nations*, New York, Alfred A. Knopf.

Ruder, David S. (1989). 'Cooperative International Securities Regulation', Remarks to the 14th Annual IOSCO Conference, Venice, 19 September.

Salomon Brothers (1990). *Multinational Money Center Banking: The Evolution of a Single Banking Market*, September.

Simpson, Thomas D. (1991). 'Trends in Global Securities Markets', in Solomon, E.H. (ed.), *Electronic Money Flows*, Dordrecht, Kluwer Academic Publishers.

Smith, Roy C. (1989). *The Global Bankers*, New York, Truman Talley Books/ Plume.

Smith, Roy C., and Walter, Ingo (1990). *Global Financial Services*, The Institutional Investor series in finance, New York, Harper Business.

Spero, Joan E. (1988-9). 'Guiding Global Finance', *Foreign Policy*, no. 73, winter.

Torres, Craig (1991). 'Bull Market for Derivatives Outruns Rules', *Wall Street Journal*, July 24.

Turner, Philip (1991). *Capital Flows in the 1980s: A Survey of Major Trends,* BIS Economic Papers, no. 30, Basle, Bank for International Settlements, April.

Walgenbach, Bernd (1990). 'International Competition between Stock Exchanges', *Intereconomics*, November/December.

Wallace, Helen, and Wilke, Marc (1990). *Subsidiarity: Approaches to Power-sharing in the European Community*, RIIA Discussion Paper no. 27, London, Royal Institute of International Affairs.

Woolcock, Stephen, Hodges, Michael, and Schreiber, Kristin (1991). *Britain, Germany and 1992: The Limits of Deregulation*, London, Royal Institute of International Affairs/Pinter.

Worthington, P.M. (1991). 'Global equity turnover: market comparisons', in *Bank of England Quarterly Bulletin*, May.